CW01237399

HOW TO WRITE
A TRAINING MANUAL

How to Write a Training Manual

John Davis

Gower
In association with
the Institute of Training and Development

© John Davis 1992

All rights reserved. No part of this publication may be reproduced, stored in a retrieval system, or transmitted in any form or by any means, electronic, mechanical, photocopying, recording, or otherwise without the permission of the publisher.

Published by
Gower Publishing Company Limited
Gower House
Croft Road
Aldershot
Hants GU11 3HR
England

Gower Publishing Company Limited
Old Post Road
Brookfield
Vermont 05036
USA

CIP catalogue records for this book are available from the British Library and the US Library of Congress

ISBN 0 566 07325 0

Typeset in 11pt Baskerville by Poole Typesetting (Wessex) Limited, Bournemouth and printed in Great Britain by Clays Ltd, Bungay.

Contents

1	**Introduction**	1
	Vive la différence?	1
	Value of preparation	3
	Aims	4
	Style of the book	4
2	**Setting up**	7
	Guidelines	9
	Thinking ahead	14
	Structure of the manual	15
3	**The rationale**	19
	Title	19
	Duration	21
	Participants	22
	Introduction	22
	Purpose	24
	Objectives	24
	Approach	27
	A little more	29
4	**Content summary**	33
	Fly on the wall	33
	How much to write?	33
	The performance appraisal example	34
	The quality customer service example	47
	The time management example	48
5	**Timetable and lists**	53
	Timetable	53
	Lists	57
	Checking back	58

6	Writing the detail	59
	The format	60
	The presentation techniques example	68
	The quality customer service example	72
	The performance appraisal example	73
7	Finally	89
	Support documentation	89
	Odds 'n ends	89
8	Using the manual	91
	Preparation	91
	Running the course	92
	Review	93

Appendix A: Presentation techniques example	95
Appendix B: Quality customer service example	105
Appendix C: Performance appraisal example	111
Index	133

List of figures

Figure 2.1	The stages involved in writing a training manual	8
Figure 2.2	Guidelines	10
Figure 2.3	Structure of the manual	17
Figure 3.1	The rationale	20
Figure 4.1	Performance appraisal mind map	35
Figure 4.2	Time management mind map	49
Figure 5.1	Example of a 'boxed' timetable	54
Figure 5.2	Preferred timetable	56

Foreword

As every trainer knows, getting the best out of any training course relies greatly on careful planning. Ensuring the defined outcomes from a course is not as easy as first imagined – especially converting creative thoughts into results. A planned progress towards the objective is essential, as John Davis explains with clarity in this book.

The reader is shown a structured approach from first thoughts, through the development stages of producing a manual, to finally using it. Reading this book should ensure that courses achieve the pre-determined objectives to a consistent quality. The style of the book is a prime example of effective training material: practical, incisive, easily assimilated and with a touch of humour.

Michael J Mitchell
Director, HRD Services Group
Institute of Training and Development

Preface

HRD is changing. It always will be if it is to be effective. However, as each new initiative or approach is introduced, much of the 'old' remains. This is particularly true of the training course. In some form or another you can bet your boots that courses will be with us for quite a while yet.

This book is about writing a trainer's manual for a training course. It is not about needs analysis, or programme development, or evaluation. It is only concerned with putting together the documentation to support effective course running.

It will not take you long to see that 'doing it this way' helps considerably in course design, but it is not about course design either.

Why bother?

There are several reasons including the need for professionalism and good planning. The most persuasive reason is that of self-interest. Prepare and write your training manual well and there is a 66.6 per cent 'guarantee' that your course will be a success! You will be so well prepared that you will be able to pay attention to the *really* important part of the business – the process.

'Doesn't everybody already do this?' you might well ask.

No. Unless we take specific courses in creative writing, or some such subject, we are not really taught how to write at school or university. We are taught how to spell (some remember), and we are taught how to write things down – but we are not really taught how to write, even though that is largely how we demonstrate whether or not we have learned anything.

That is why we see so many – conduct so many – report writing and business letter writing courses. Often it is assumed that because you can talk fluently about something you can write about it with the same ease and skill. But we know that it is not so. Often when we try, we find it terribly hard to write about what we are quite comfortable speaking about. Almost as often we avoid it.

Well, as far as a training manual is concerned, it is well worth the extra effort – and you will improve with practice. You will achieve your objectives more certainly. In addition, sharpen this skill and you will sharpen your other training skills: needs analysis, objective writing, material research, structure development, programme evaluation and, above all, process management.

A good training manual is evidence of and an aid to:

- thinking;
- programme and personal development;
- training effectiveness.

To me, that would seem a great return on your invested effort.

John Davis

1 Introduction

If you are a training manager and you want to help develop your team's professionalism, this book can help. If you want to base discussions with your trainers about their courses on something concrete rather than abstract, this process will work.

If you are a trainer and you would like to make sure you are adequately prepared, this can help. If you would like a process that helps you better to control all aspects of your courses, this may be it.

If you write material for others to deliver, and you do not use a similar process, you should.

VIVE LA DIFFÉRENCE

There are many ways to write a training manual: more than there are actual trainers. There is no single best way, and few really good ways either! All trainers write training material a little differently. It is disconcerting that quite often individual trainers write differently each time they write.

Why 'disconcerting'?

Let us look at some of the possible reasons we might change the way we write our next training manual, and the next, and the next, and the next . . . .

- 'It's a different course, so it needs a different approach.'
- 'I didn't like the way it went last time; I have to make some changes.'
- 'I couldn't understand what I'd written.'
- They weren't really my notes anyway, I copied most of them.'
- 'There isn't any good reason not to change.'
- 'I lost my notes, or someone borrowed them.'

I could list more. So could you. None of them really hold much water.

The format described in this book emerged slowly from a sort of 'primaeval jungle' of early training experiences; some good, most not so good. It was a result of survival, discovery, development, trial and many errors, and redevelopment. No doubt there is *still* plenty of room for improvement. Those early experiences were full of uncertainty about how I should proceed in my new line of work. No one told me how to marshal information and put it in a useable form. They had managed on their own, so could I. I did get some occasional help; I could sometimes borrow someone else's notes, though that was never as much help as I might have hoped.

Training material was developed from a little reading, a pinch of your own ideas, a smidgen of discussion and 'extracts' from other people's work. When that was all put together you had your course notes. And that is all you had – course notes. By no stretch of the imagination could it be called proper documentation.

It was worse when you had to take over someone else's course and work from *their* notes. They almost always included gems like:

- 'Discuss motivation with the group.'
- 'Discuss the importance of good preparation in communication.'
- Get the group to agree the three most important factors of good leadership.'

How? What aspects? For how long? To what end? Certainly the paucity of these course notes prompted you to do your own research. You had to discuss important questions with others. While that is good, it is not reason enough for putting up with poor documentation. There are better, more certain ways to develop the talents and abilities of trainers.

Whenever I asked why there was no standard way of producing the material I was told that each trainer liked to do things in his or her own way. You could not force people into writing course material in the same way. It would stifle their creativity. And that, I believe, was an excuse for not wanting to make the effort to change. There is a world of difference between forcing people to do things against their will and providing a sound format to help them become better trainers.

All of these different, highly personal forms of course documentation are to a professional approach what graffiti is to art. It is sort of OK sometimes, but . . . .

Training is communication. Without good quality and thorough preparation the communication will falter; it will achieve less than what is possible. Good quality training documentation is part of that preparation. It will leave no room for questions of 'How?' 'What aspects?' 'How long for?' and 'To what end?'

Yet another concern grew when I worked with other trainers. Often I would notice that material was delivered in a different way each time the trainer worked with groups of learners. When I asked why, the standard response was that the group was different. My own observations told me that this was not the real reason. Trainers were 'winging it' – making it up as they went along. In the early days I found this very impressive. Would I, I wondered, ever be as clever as these knowledgeable gurus?

They knew what they were talking about and felt confident that learners were getting good value. And they were, but each group was getting *different* material. This is fine if it is planned, or in specific response to learner needs, but often enough this was not the case. The approach lacked discipline – an essential ingredient of a professional in any line of work.

Imagine what would happen if the medical profession made things up in the same way. How would you feel under the surgeon's knife if you knew the 'manual' from which he or she was working was somewhat vague on this particular type of operation, and half-way through the surgeon was 'going to try something a little different this time?' How would doctors learn from others? How would they pass that learning on to yet other doctors without the discipline of making changes through planning *followed by* professional response? Would you, the patient, survive?

VALUE OF PREPARATION

If you are redecorating a room at home it makes sense to prepare. Move furniture out, cover what you cannot move, ensure brushes and tins are clean, and so on. I know a few people who just want to get on with the painting, and the preparation part is given short shrift or left undone. It is a bit risky, but if they are careful they can get by – do a reasonable job.

A trainer needs three things to be effective in running a course.

- much more knowledge of the subject than is actually being documented and delivered;
- consummate delivery skills;
- good delivery supports, including top quality documentation.

You can get by on any two out of three. If that is all you want – to get by – and you know your material and you are good 'up front', you do not need a well prepared, disciplined, repeatable, fully comprehensible training manual. If you want more than just to get by, you do.

The format described in this book was developed over a number of years with the help of a number of people. It was tested hundreds of times. It was applied in organizations in which I worked. It works.

The format makes much clearer things such as total content, meaning, time and timing, pace, delivery style and expectations. It assures more than adequate trainer preparation. It gives a rock-solid foundation for change or improvement. You know precisely what you are starting with. You can pinpoint what needs changing, and you can change only the parts that really need it. You can judge the total impact of any modification *before* testing it on learner victims.

Often you do need to modify a programme in response to learners' needs. Whether this is before or during the programme the format can help to show what else you have to think about. What else needs changing? What needs adding or deleting? What is the impact on time? What about the learning objectives? Impact can be controlled, other changes planned in advanced, and the quality of the experience maintained or improved.

This is certainly better than the sweating palms, rising blood pressure and silent prayers to the patron saint of trainers (Saint Olaf the Hopeful) when learner-group pressures steer a course away from where you were heading and you have no mechanism for knowing where the heck you are going to wind up!

The format also helps trainers deliver materials developed by others without the pain of wondering what the writers actually mean. It can help non-trainers understand not only the 'what', but the 'why' and 'how' of delivery when they have to get involved in delivering training.

The format does not extend the time needed for programme development. It is a way of focusing the development process clearly on the end goal. It becomes easier to make decisions about what to put in or leave out, or how to deal with a topic.

When you have finished writing the training manual you will have further developed your own skills and understanding. You will be absolutely prepared for a star performance in the training room. That has to be worth the effort.

AIMS

I have no way of testing your learning as a reader of this book. So I will not set learning objectives. I can and should say what my aims are though. In this way you can read what follows with a little more direction. You will be the judge of whether I achieve them or not.

My aims then, are that after reading this book you will:

- want to improve your training course documentation;
- be able to apply the format described;
- further 'study', work with and discuss the contents of the book with colleagues;
- adopt and use the format;
- run better courses;
- help others to develop more effective preparation and delivery skills.

A tall order, but if I can achieve the first two aims the third and fourth are likely to be achieved also. Certainly the process is straightforward, but it does take some effort to make it work. If the first four aims are achieved, you will run better courses. You will know it, and so will your trainees. I am sure that under those circumstances you will want to pass on your skills to help others in the same way.

STYLE OF THE BOOK

The book has examples throughout. Some of these illustrate how to improve what I have already written. But please remember, that is the way I thought changes were needed at the time. Certainly these could be further improved. If you think you can improve them – be my guest. I promise that you will not hurt my feelings.

These examples appear in the form of layout you might find in a training manual (normally made up of ring binder and A4 size paper). In some examples the text is smaller or there is less space than you might expect to find in a training manual in order to fit on a page of this book.

Wherever possible I have used illustrations or diagrams to help emphasize or make a point, or maybe just for fun. They are intended as useful summaries of what is written. If they do not make sense to you, talk about them with someone else, or just ignore them.

There is a generous amount of space in the book; use this to write your own comments or margin notes. It helps the memory, and it can help to vent any

Introduction

frustrations I might cause. (If it is not your own book, do not do it. Write on your own paper or buy your own book!)

From time to time in the early pages we will check back. I will ask you, the reader to do something – answer a question, or write something down. Ignore this if you like, but it will be better if you participate actively whenever you can.

Above all you have to *work with* the material. If you differ or disagree with me, then argue your point as if I am there. Try to work out what I would say in response to you. Often, I will ask you to close your eyes and visualize what is happening; to 'feel' your way through some work; to look for balance. Try it. If you can manage it, it can really pay off. This is not an academic exercise. It is a practical guide for practical people. Its worth will not become really clear until you have tried the format – really tried it – in actual training.

No let us try a couple of easy questions; just to sum up two main points, for practice, and a bit of fun. For the sake of ease the answer is alternative (c) for both questions. If you are tempted to choose any other answer you should:

(a) throw away the book;
(b) get a job as a politician;
(c) re-evaluate your choice of career;
(d) all of the above.

1   How did the training manual format described in this book come about?

   (a) It was invented by God.

   (b) It was discovered in a Roman Army training manual circa 98BC.

   (c) It was through many years training experience, discovery, trial, error and finding out what actually works in practice.

   (d) It is still a mystery to you.

2   Why should you seriously consider giving this format a real try?

   (a) If you do not your nose will rot and drop off.

   (b) If you do you will win a pot full of gold.

   (c) It really can help to develop greater professionalism and effectiveness.

   (d) Because I am a really nice person and you do not want to upset me with such an awful rejection.

2 Setting up

The following pages describe each of the stages involved in writing a training manual. Figure 2.1 summarizes the process. It will help to give a quick overview – and should be kept in mind when working through this chapter.

The process starts when learning needs have been identified, a training course is perceived to be the answer, and its objectives have been agreed with the client/s.

The first stage is writing the course outline. Here you describe (in summary form) what the learning experience is, what it will achieve, what it will be like, what it covers, and about how long it will take. This stage involves setting your ideas down quickly; to write enough to give a clear indication of all that is involved, but to be brief enough to be able to grasp the whole experience in one quick reading or discussion – *without getting lost in detail*.

The course outline is what you take to clients. It is basis from which you craft the finished course. Once your ideas have been confirmed you can get down to writing the course out in detail.

This is where you determine what you will say and do: your key points, how you will deliver them; how these will be supported by visuals, films, exercises, and so on. It is the stage where the purpose, content, style and timing of all materials, visuals, exercises, syndicate tasks and case studies are finalized (more or less) and documented.

The next stage is to make sure that nothing you have written, read or referenced is lost. You pull all the information and documentation together. You marshall (and store in your manual) all your master documents (syndicate exercises, case studies), references, bibliography and so on.

The final stage is to prepare for the course. Do this as close to the actual running of the course as you can. That way it is fresh in your memory. On the other hand you need to have enough time to make some final changes if you decide you need to.

In this last stage work through the whole manual, especially the detailed text. Decide what requires special emphasis, familiarize yourself with the timing, practise key phrases, setting up syndicate exercises and so on. Road test parts of the course on colleagues, unsuspecting friends, or just the mirror. Get ready.

Figure 2.1 The stages involved in writing a training manual

```
                    ╭─────────╮
                    │  Needs  │
                    │identified│
                    ╰─────────╯
                         ↑    ╭──────────╮
                         │    │Objectives│
                         │    │  agreed  │
                         │    ╰──────────╯
                         │         │
                         │         ↓
  R                      │   ┌──────────────┐     Guidelines
  e                      │   │ WRITE COURSE │ ←── Objectives
  s                      │   │   OUTLINE    │     Approach/style
                         │   └──────────────┘     Content summary
                         │         │              Timeframes
                         │         ↓
                         │   ┌──────────────┐
                         └───│  CHECK WITH  │
                             │   CLIENTS    │
                             └──────────────┘
  e                                │
  a                                ↓              Guidelines
                             ┌──────────────┐     Pre-work
                         ┌──→│ WRITE DETAIL │───→ Text
                         │   └──────────────┘     Visuals
                         │          │             Exercises
                         │          │             Case studies
                         │          │             Films/Videos
                         │          │             Other facilities/
                         │          │                information
                         │          ↓
                         │   ┌──────────────────┐
                         │   │ MARSHALL SUPPORT │
  r                      │   │  INFORMATION AND │
                         │   │OTHER ODDS AND ENDS│
                         │   └──────────────────┘
                         │          │
                         │          ↓
                         │   ┌──────────────┐     Work through
                         │   │ PREPARE FOR  │     Emphasis
                         └───│  THE COURSE  │     Timing
  c                          └──────────────┘     Road test
  h
```

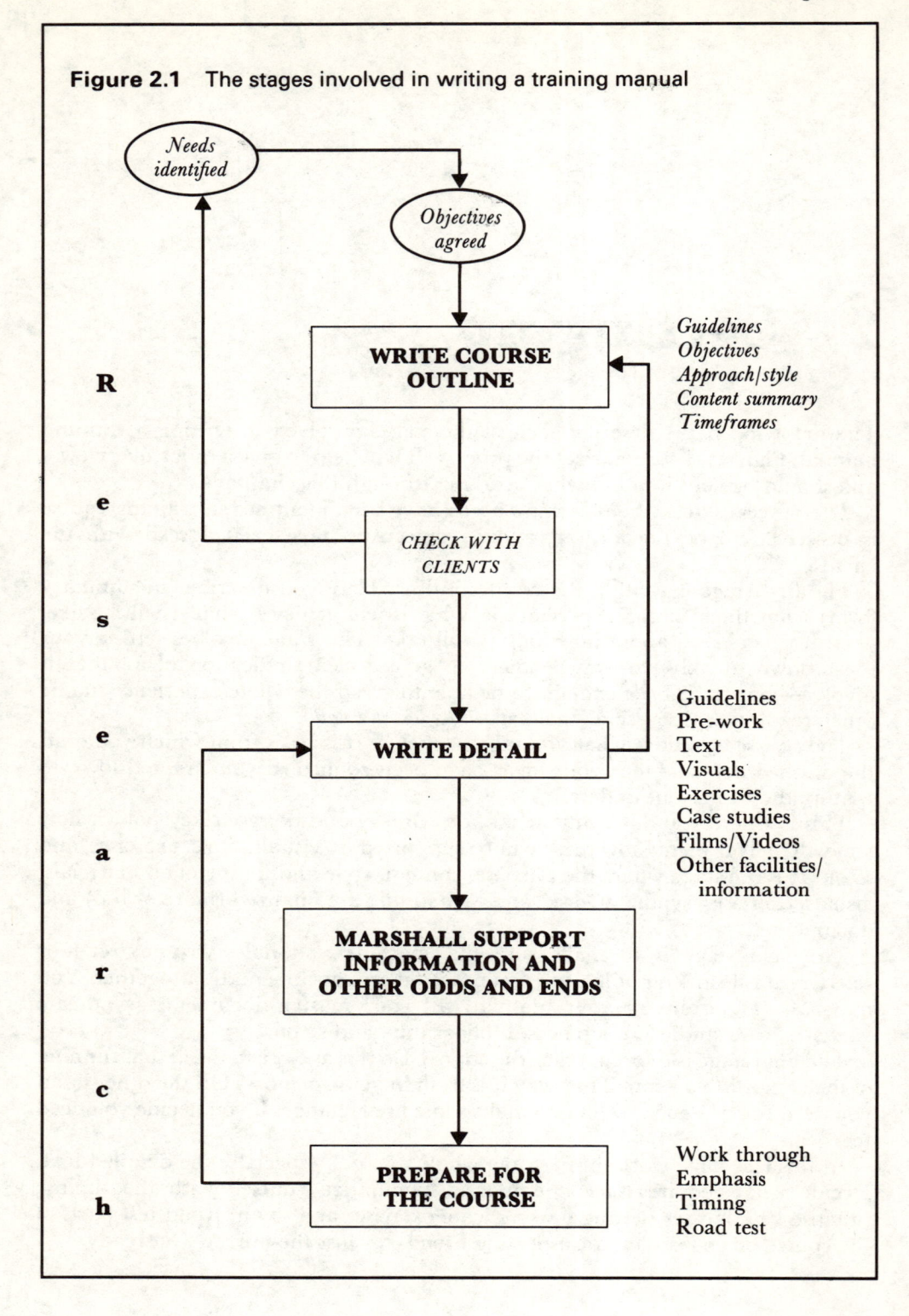

Now, before I describe what to do in more detail, we will look at the following:

- '*Guidelines*' – thoughts that might help you to do a good job;
- '*Thinking ahead*' – what you need to think about when developing your course; and
- '*Structure of the Manual*' – the way it is assembled.

GUIDELINES

Following the guidelines will lead to successful manual writing. Remember, though, that they are guidelines and not rules. Ignoring or modifying guidelines should be a matter of shared policy, that is everyone in the same training team must follow the same guidelines. Idiosyncrasy must be subordinated to discipline. If people tinker with the format on an individual basis then an invaluable asset is lost – understanding of the what, why, where when and how of a training course regardless of who actually developed it, and regardless of who normally runs it.

The guidelines themselves are written in a way that challenges thinking. Some explanation will be given here, but there is still a need for people to think through and feel for their own meaning (see Figure 2.2).

Write for someone else, not for yourself

It is fashionable in some areas to separate the writing of training courses from their actual delivery. The idea may have a sound basis. At times it may be unavoidable. For me, it lacks something. Those who deliver training courses really experience and *feel* what works and what does not. To try to pass that on to writers who have not shared the delivery experience can be an exercise in futility. You know the old phrase – 'you had to be there'.

Conversely, presenters who cannot involve themselves in subject research, the collection, rejection and selection of material do not understand the material in the way that the writer intends. And skilled presenters who cannot construct their ideas beforehand or who cannot write are unlikely to fulfil the complete role of trainer. Flair is no substitute for professionalism.

Notwithstanding its title, this guideline is written on the basis that if you write the training manual you will run the course. But write for someone else for the following reasons:

- When you make your course notes, there is always the temptation to assume you will remember precisely what you mean (when writing key words or phrases) at a later date. But if you do not explain things fully to yourself when you write you will probably forget. You will wind up with 'discuss motivation with the group', and have to make things up as you go along. The manual is supposed to prevent the need for that.
- Your writing should be like a careful explanation to someone else of your material and the thinking behind it. There should be no remaining questions of intent or meaning. If you cannot explain it to yourself how will you explain it to someone else?

Figure 2.2 Guidelines

- Write for someone else, not for yourself.
- You must know the structure and sequence, and how to use it.
- Get your learning/training objectives right, right away.
- Write your 'text' in spoken English and do not be constrained by the rules of grammar.
- Everybody should follow the same format.
- Everybody should use the format when training.
- When you are writing, think of the theme music.
- No guideline is inviolate, but think hard before setting one aside.

Setting up

- Writing for 'someone else' will help you to see things from another perspective. You are less likely to make assumptions about how others will understand your material when you deliver it. When a learner asks 'why' you'll be well prepared.
- One day it is going to happen: someone else will have to deliver your material. You'll be sick, or on leave, or kidnapped by jealous colleagues, or just promoted out of your position and someone else is going to have to deliver *your* material. Do you want them to mess it up? Or do you want them to deliver it *exactly* as you intended? How will your feel about your baby?

You must know the structure and sequence, and how to use it

The manual is written in a number of sequential steps that might be numbered 1, 2, 3, 4, 5 and so on. Of course it makes sense to start at the beginning, at step 1, then move on through the sequence. Unfortunately it is not always possible.

We may get writer's block (a sort of mental constipation), or some important information is missing, or you want to try something new. The reasons are numerous. When a problem occurs you can skip steps – start drafting a few visuals, write a few lines of text, construct a handout – do anything to get yourself moving.

Sooner or later though, you are going to have to tidy things up. If you know the structure inside out your will not leave things half done.

Get your learning/training objectives right, right away

I do not know how many people 'buy' training, or attend courses without a clear understanding of how the training will affect them when they finish. Quite a few, I suspect. I do not know how many training courses are written without a clear idea of what they are supposed to achieve, or how we will know when it has been achieved. Again, quite a few probably.

The situation certainly needs improvement. What is pertinent here though is what it means for writing a good training manual. You have to know where you are going before you start. There is only one virtue in not knowing and that is you never know when you are lost. Not much of virtue, is it?

If your objectives are not written down you cannot be sure you are writing for the right end. You cannot be sure you are writing the right material.

So – the next time you are asked to 'develop a short course on communication for managers', do not start until the objectives are written down (and agreed). When they are you will know where you are headed.

Write your 'text' in spoken English, and do not be constrained by the rules of grammar

'Text' is what you are actually going to say to your trainees (more or less). It is the padding around your key words, ideas and phrases that makes them understandable because it is the way you would explain them to your trainees. When you *do* actually work from your text you will probably change the words you use – after all you won't be reading from a script. (More about that later.)

So – why write text in spoken English? Have you ever listened to a presentation in written English? Does it not sound turgid? When you are writing your manual use the spoken word: imagine yourself actually speaking to your trainees in the language you would normally use, and write that.

What about not being constrained by the rules of grammar? You might need to forget commas or full stops; leave the inverted commas from nicknames; break sentences in the middle with a paragraph-type space. You need to use layout and spacing so that the material can, in the first place, talk to you. You will need to bend the rules sometimes for that to happen. Here is a short example.

WE NOW COME TO THE FINAL ELEMENT OF OUR 'COMMUNICATIONS' SEGMENT. WE WILL NOW DEAL WITH 'MAKING A PRESENTATION'. AS MANAGERS YOU WILL OFTEN FIND YOURSELVES IN SITUATIONS WHERE YOU WILL HAVE TO SELL, OR PERSUADE, OR PROMOTE SOMETHING THROUGH SOME FORM OF PRESENTATION, WHETHER THIS BE THROUGH REGIONAL OR NATIONAL CONFERENCES, OR PROFESSIONAL PUBLIC APPEARANCES.

This might talk to you more as . . .

OK – WE'RE NOW GOING TO DEAL WITH THE LAST BIT OF OUR COMMUNICATIONS SEGMENT.

WE'RE GOING TO COVER PRESENTATIONS.

MANAGERS LIKE YOU WILL OFTEN FIND YOURSELVES IN SITUATIONS WHERE YOU HAVE TO SELL OR PERSUADE OR PROMOTE SOMETHING THROUGH SOME FORM OF PRESENTATION.

THIS MIGHT BE AT A COMPANY CONFERENCE AT REGIONAL OR NATIONAL LEVEL.

OR IT MIGHT BE SPEAKING TO YOUR PROFESSIONAL BODY.

ANY 'PUBLIC APPEARANCE' – YOU'LL BE ON DISPLAY.

This will be covered in more detail later, but for now I hope the second example has had more of an impact; showing how the use of space can send messages to your eye about delivery, and how the rigid application of 'correct grammatical English' would interfere with getting the message 'to us, through us, to them'.

Everybody should follow the same format

Within your own team modify whatever you like. Make up your own team guidelines, your own team format. Everyone in the team should then apply their own creativity within that same disciplined format. You can then discuss apples with apples with apples when you need to.

Different people can work on different parts of the same project and it will still hang together as a nice tidy whole. Anyone within the team will be able to understand the work of others within the team because they are working with the same format.

But trainers are trainers. We are infamous for believing infinite creativity and individuality is an inalienable right! It takes some management, but it's worth the effort.

Everybody should use the format when training

I introduced this format in a training team I once had the pleasure of working with. Everyone agreed it was a good idea, (really). Still, one day I noticed one of my trainers working with another form of rough, personal notes.

The format was designed for practical benefit – to be used, not just in the design stage, but also in delivery. The trainer still felt 'safer' with the 'old style' of notes. It sometimes takes a little effort to sell the benefits. It sometimes takes quite a bit of persistence before the benefits are realized. So persist.

When you are writing, think of the theme music

I imagine that, like me, you have seen some desperately woeful trainers in action. Some seem to think they have a God-given right to bore the pants off their trainees. Others seem to think that entertainment is a substitute for substance. Training is not entertainment, but it should be entertaining, or at least interesting enough for people to want more. We must always consider how we can develop and maintain the interest of our trainees.

This can be done at the outset, when we begin to develop our programme.

How can we introduce drama, impact, interest? How can we do that without gimmicks ('always start your session with a joke' – ugh!) or tricks? How can we best construct the learning experience, the dialogue between trainer and trainee? How do we keep momentum throughout? These are questions which must be answered in the development stage, when you are writing your training manual.

How does Hollywood do it? Writing good theme music is one way. Now I am *not* saying that you should bring an orchestra into the training room. Imagine the chaos of doing things while working at close quarters with quivering violin bows and jabbing baton. Anyway the theme music is added when everything else is finished – but there is a lesson to be learned. Hollywood does not leave it at a good script, and good actors – that is enough. It looks for ways to enhance the experience for its audience. What can you do to add value?

We must think about the whole experience from the trainees' point of view. How will they *experience*, feel, respond and react to what you deliver? What will make it interesting and entertaining as well as valuable? If you cannot answer that, value may not follow at all.

No guideline is inviolate, but think hard before setting one aside

As I said before, they are not rules, only guides to success. However, they do comprise a complete framework within which to work. Even so, there must be room for improvement – there always is. Keep working at it.

THINKING AHEAD

This book assumes that you will be writing a training manual in response to defined needs, so we will not dwell on that – except to say that sometimes it is not as easy as it seems. For instance: a group of senior managers asked me to develop a course for their subordinate managers. The topic was an area that was fundamental to the business of the organization. They (the managers) had been involved in this kind of work for absolutely ever. It required hardly any genius at all to determine that there was some sort of problem to be solved. We agreed on two.

First, the managers had never been formally trained (off the job), even in the basics, and second, the world in which they were carrying out the work had undergone some considerable change.

The course was to cover the basic principles behind the work. They did not need any technical skilling. (Remember, they had been doing 'this kind of work for absolutely ever'.) We needed to concentrate on the human interaction between the managers and their 'customers'. The senior managers agreed and endorsed this. We agreed the specific objectives. I wrote the course, discussed it with the senior managers, and they said it was what they wanted.

We ran the course, and it was not successful. It was beautifully written, and I ran it well (naturally), and it was unsuccessful. My customers – the trainees – did not like it. The senior managers did not like it. *They* all agreed that *we had* got it wrong, and of course we had. Even though I did not like it I had to admit that it was really my fault.

What they needed in fact were some basic technical skills, dressed up in a way that looked more advanced, more acceptable to the trainees themselves. No one had told them they were not doing their jobs well enough. No one wanted to admit that to me – a trainer.

There were other factors involved, but that is the basic sad story. We had done the wrong thing in the right way. We had wasted time, money and energy. We had lost credibility. The lesson? You can do a great job with the manual and fail – and it will not be the manual or even your delivery skills. If you write the wrong information for the wrong people, you will have problems.

So too, 'objectives'. Writing a training manual starts from the point where objectives have been agreed and the manual can be written around them. If only it were that simple! I am still a little surprised to find that few people can write good training/learning objectives. Only a little, because although there is not much writing involved, it is an exceptionally difficult task to formulate good objectives. It takes more practice, skill, dedication and time than we often have available.

If you want to know how your objective writing measures up, read Robert Mager's *Preparing Instructional Objectives* (2nd edn. 1984, Lake Management & Training, Belmont, USA). It is a good book and I wish I had written it.

When you encounter 'objectives' in this book I will be skipping lightly over the subject. I will also be touching on heresy, most probably. Still, my conscience is clear. I have told you where to look for quality information on the subject.

In talking about 'needs' and 'objectives' I have touched on some of the uncomfortable realities of the world in which we work. And there are more. Trainers cannot exist in a cocoon. We have to take the wider view of our world, and keep that in mind when we work. For instance, before you start your manual you have to take account of some important factors.

For whom else are you writing? There are your 'customers' the trainees, their bosses or nominators, other trainers who may have to work with you and your material, and of course, your training manager. What are they expecting? What would they like to see? What questions will they have that you can answer in your manual before they ask?

Even if you are a lone operator you are going to have to sell your course to someone before it runs. You will do that with the outline – *if* you take account of important others and write accordingly. Let us take an easy 'for instance'.

For instance, you will know what words, phrases, ideas and approaches your training manager likes or dislikes. Take them into account. That does not mean that you have to put in, or leave out things according to these tastes. It means you take them into account. There are costs and benefits involved when deciding your approach. Know what they are, and what you are prepared to 'pay'.

You need to know what other needs and goals must be serviced by your manual. Will any part of it be used to publicize your course? If the answer is 'Yes', then you need to know the sort of language that will serve this purpose as well as that of helping you to prepare for a great course.

Do you need acceptance from other quarters? Are you selling your own value as well as the course? Is the job also reinforcing reputation? Write accordingly.

Think about style. Make sure each word you use earns its place. We will not be perfect, but we can try, and in the trying, be better.

Take the view that you are writing a story. Give it purpose and drama. Make it interesting for someone else. You will find it becomes interesting for you. I doubt that anyone would expect the results of your writing labour to resemble the work of Tolstoy or Dickens, Forsyth or Clavell, nor should you, but why not try to put quality and interest in your work?

Write as if someone else is going to write the detail from your outline. Make sure that they can do a superb job. You'll find that it will increase your chances of doing the same. And remember – you cannot please everybody, but you can give it your best shot.

STRUCTURE OF THE MANUAL

The structure of the manual has a logic intended to lead you from your initial thinking about the course, through the planning and development stages, the collection of data and materials to be used, to the end process of writing the manual in detail. It is intended to help keep you focused and on track.

It provides a means of exploring and distilling your ideas about a training experience – in writing the outline – which improves the final quality of the course. When you discuss your ideas with colleagues you have them written down; there is something real and concrete to discuss. It becomes an aid to creativity ('why not try to do that using this . . .') and an insurance against inappropriate content or style ('hang on, if you do that – will it really fit?').

The structure can help in the research stage of course design. You can begin to write a course outline before you complete your research into appropriate information, methods and styles. It provides a means by which you can test out where you need further to develop (your information, your knowledge and understanding of the topic, your skills).

The format asks that you commit your ideas and thoughts in writing at an early stage in the overall development process. You do not lose or forget what you intended or where you were going. It encourages review and evaluation at all stages of development. It insures against inflicting completely untested 'experiments' on unsuspecting trainees.

Clearly there are many benefits, but they are not without cost. It demands discipline, the ability to write, the ability to do at least a modicum of research, empathy for trainees, and the professional commitment to thorough preparation. It is hard, but rewarding work.

The structure of the manual is outlined in Figure 2.3. What I would like to do first is quickly sketch in the whole of the structure, then deal with each of its sections in turn, giving some examples of how it should work. Do not get hung up on the titles I use for things. It is the format or process that is important. If you do not like the specific words I use, choose some you do like, but *participate*.

Remember that the outline is a complete summary of each aspect of the course. A quick reading of it should help to get an immediate understanding of who it is for, what it is about, what it includes and what it involves. It would be just *possible* (not desirable) to run the course from the outline itself. There should be enough information there for the skilled trainer, thoroughly familiar with the topic, to get through the experience. Time spent here, thinking through, and writing quality material, is time very well spent.

If you are not *perfectly* skilled, and *absolutely* familiar with *all* aspects of the topic, leave yourself no choice but to invest heavily in getting this right.

The outline points the way and uncovers the reasoning for the whole course. It has four sections:

- the rationale;
- the content summary;
- the timetable;
- lists.

The rationale sets up the outline, showing what is to follow. It is to tell people what the event is, what it is about, and who it is for. The content summary is clearly the main part of the outline. It describes what is to be covered, and how content will be treated. The timetable shows how much time is supposed to be spent in the various parts of the course. It outlines what is dealt with, when. It includes key information relating to visuals, handouts and exercises. The lists do just that. They list what else you will need to run the course.

Figure 2.3 Structure of the manual

| **OUTLINE** | Rationale
Content summary
Timetable
Lists |

| **DETAIL** | Text
Trainer notes
Visuals |

| **SUPPORT DOCUMENTATION** | Handout masters
Extracts masters
Syndicate/Group exercises masters
Case study masters
Other support papers |

| **ODDS 'n ENDS** | References
Bibliography
Any other relevant material or data |

The second part is the detail of the course. This includes:

- the 'text' and trainer notes;
- visual aids.

The third part includes all the 'master' documents for the course such as:

- visuals' masters;
- handouts;
- syndicate/group exercises briefs;
- any other 'support papers'.

The final part of the manual is an 'odds 'n ends' category, which includes any other important data (such as development, or research references) which do not 'fit' into any other part of the manual. It is all fairly straightforward really.

In all, each section provides a different kind of summary of the course, showing the course from different perspectives. Each of these helps the writer, and ultimately the trainer, to keep in mind the whole experience without getting lost in the detail.

Further, they test out, at the design stage, the balance, legitimacy and logic of the course and really help you to get a feel for what is right for the experience.

The structure provides a framework that allows you to start or work on whatever part you like: wherever you feel most comfortable or confident. But before we move on to a more detailed description though, let us see how we are doing.

All right, sit up straight, and take a deep breath. Here are a few easy questions to help you decide what you need to do next.

1   Can you list all eight of the guidelines? (A 'Yes' or 'No' answer is not good enough. You actually have to write them down.)
2   What has Hollywood to do with writing your training manual?
3   At what stage must you always begin when writing your manual?
4   Give two reasons why a trainer's individuality and creativity should be kept within the same format?
5   What was your mother's maiden name?
6   How many separate parts of the manual are there?
7   What is the last part called, and what is it for?

How did you do? Remember I said that you would have to work with the material, not just be a passive reader of it? If you did not do too well, perhaps you would benefit from skipping through the material again. At any rate you must have at least one of the answers right!

3 The rationale

Figure 3.1 shows the contents of the rationale. It serves at least three purposes. It provides information about the course, it can be used as publicity, and it is a starting point – something that helps you to get going with the writing job.

If someone (a potential user of the course, nominating manager, or your manager) reads only the rationale, he or she will still have some information and understanding of what it is about. This may help you to focus initial discussions about the course – with your manager, or prospective user – before you get too deeply into its development.

The rationale, or an edited version of it, can be used to publicize your course, in a course/programme brochure for instance and so because of this potential usage you should give it some serious and creative thought. You do not get a second chance to make a first impression. If it is to be used as publicity then you may want to include an indication of content. I do not normally include it. The rationale helps me write the manual. At this stage of writing I would not have decided on the final contents. If you need to show content in the rationale, you can add it later, when you have finished writing the whole manual.

The rationale should be one, or at most two A4 pages long, but some unusual programmes may call for more. The aim is to embark on the business of writing the material as quickly as possible, so keep it brief. The rationale should quickly *grab* the interest of whoever is going to read your material, so keep it brief.

Many people find creative writing difficult. Even some trainers! Starting with the rationale can make it easier. Apart from writing the objectives it is all pretty easy stuff. Let us go through the rationale step by step.

TITLE

Make the title punchy as well as informative. It is the first opportunity you have to interest someone – or turn them off. Make it work with impact in your environment. If you're in a somewhat conservative organization then the title 'Stand Up, Speak Well', may not work as well as 'Presentation Skills'.

A friend of mine used the title 'Imageering' for his oral presentation skills course. The title was intriguing, and gave some hint of how the subject would

Figure 3.1 The rationale

TITLE	*Make it work for you. Be creative.*
DURATION	*How long would I be away from work?*
PARTICIPANTS	*Is this aimed at me anyway?*
INTRODUCTION	*What is it really about?*
PURPOSE	*Why should I bother?*
OBJECTIVES	*What will I get out of it?*
APPROACH	*What will it be like?*

be treated; some indication of the importance of creating the right sort of image. I think he got off to a really good start.

If you need to, you can always subtitle your course. For example:

IMAGEERING

A presentation skills course for senior managers

STAND UP, SPEAK WELL

How to build effective public speaking skills

Certainly, in some organizations this might seem a bit over the top. It might be better to label a course 'Presentation Skills', or 'Public Speaking' or something else that is more in keeping with stiff collars, quill pens and all the adventure of a walk around your back yard.

Further examples might be:

SOLUTIONS THAT WORK

A practical problem-solving course for supervisors

YOU, YOUR TEAM AND SUCCESS

Team leadership and team work programme for managers

Again, more acceptable and effective titles might be 'Practical Problem Solving', and 'Team Leadership'. In the end event you will know the better approach for your purposes. You will know whether some razzle dazzle will enhance your cause or bring on a charge of flippancy. Still, if you can find an effective, dynamic title (even if you are the only one who ever reads it) it will give you more of a feel for what you want to write, and the way you want to write it. You must strive to create images with your words. If you do, what you write will not be forgotten. Do not write anything without thinking about it – even the title of your course.

DURATION

It would be comforting to believe that once needs had been properly analysed and objectives agreed we would simply design a course and then see how long it is. I suppose it can happen like that sometimes. Unfortunately we are more often than not both constrained and controlled by time. People are interested in how long it is going to take at least as much as how much they might learn (that is why they will keep on turning up to two-day courses which promise to teach them all they need to know about supervisory or communication skills.) Time is an important business resource and one we need to keep in mind.

The first question many ask, when they have the answer to 'What is it?' is 'How long would I be away from work?' So tell them.

PARTICIPANTS

The next question that is likely to be asked – if interest is still there – is 'Is this really for me?'

In many organizations this is given. Needs analysis starts (and unfortunately, too often ends) with something like 'I want you to run a course for my managers in communication'. Whatever the case, be as specific as you can when providing this piece of information. Do not forget, this is to help you develop the right course for the right people. After all, you probably would not develop quite the same communications skills course for a group of blue collar Knockers and Fettlers' shop stewards as you would for TV announcers.

What we have for the first three elements of the rationale can be seen as the 'flag' that you wave to get people's attention, for example, 'Report Writing, a two-day course for Supervising Engineers'.

INTRODUCTION

The Introduction comes next. This is your first real opportunity to clear your mind, write something and direct your development work. It should address the question 'Why?'

For instance, let us suppose I am just beginning to develop a short course on performance appraisal. The company has a 'sort of' system that does not really work, and will be introducing a new system in the near future. Before that happens it wants its managers made aware of the issues involved, and 'skilled up'. (Discussion would probably be about that vague.) We have agreed that the company's 12 senior managers will be trained first so that they can:

- determine with their managers the perceived problems with the existing system;
- contribute to the development of an improved system;
- coach and counsel their managers, when the new system is introduced, and identify priorities for action, including identifying who needs training.
- be able to appraise the performance of their subordinate managers.

Obviously the customers (senior managers) occupy key positions. We cannot take them away from the job for long. I can have them (I have been told) for only two days. We have agreed that I will probably be able to have them back for more training in the new system – 'if they need it' – when the new system's been finally developed. I have got a week to get back with a proposal. I am going to write my outline, and sell that.

My introduction would look something like this.

> Performance Appraisal is worth covering in any programme of management development. There are two principal reasons. The first is that an organization's success depends on how well its employees carry out their work. Someone has to make judgements about that. The more disciplined and accurate those judgements are, the better the results of feedback and corrective action will be. The second reason is that the activity of appraising performance can be conflict-ridden. Even if it were easy to understand it would still be difficult to do well.

No doubt that could be improved. We could take out some of the long words; sharpen up ideas; shorten some of the sentences. And we would for the finished document, but what does that tell us so far? What help does it give us in writing the manual?

Well – I am trying to establish the importance of appraisal. I want my trainees to agree that it is one of their key responsibilities. (If they do not, they will not be all that interested, will they?) I also want to explore the problems with appraisal so that they *can* contribute to developing a better system. I want them to manage the inevitable conflicts that performance appraisal gives rise to.

They are going to require *some* skills training if they are to 'coach and counsel' their subordinate managers, but I am going to leave the 'real' appraisal skills development until we have a new system – so I make no mention of it in the introduction.

My introduction helps me to focus on what else I might put into this course.

What about an introduction for a course for time management?

Let us suppose that it has been decided that time management skills are lacking in the organization, and that these skills are seen as important for managers. We have had our discussions, and my brief is to develop a short course (again) that will be job relevant and practical, the results of which can be followed up – that is measured.

Let us say . . . I have done some research into the subject, but not much. . . . I have not had time to research the problems in the organization as perceived by the intended trainees. . . . 'Relevance' will be something to be built in by the participants themselves. . . . I have got the title of the course, (cleverly called 'Time Management'). It is for the company's managers at any level. . . . I have skipped the question of 'duration' because so far I do not know how long this will take, and I am sitting at my desk wondering where the heck to start. So . . . .

> A manager 'manages' many things: people, situations, resources. Always among the scarcest of resources is time. If that is not managed properly everything else is more difficult. This course will provide some practical actions that managers can take to make sure their time is used as productively as possible.

There – it is done. I have kept it brief and crisp, in line with a feeling for the topic. I have legitimized the topic as an essential element of managerial responsibility.

I have suggested that regardless of changes in the organization or manager's job the 'time' problem will not go away. I have set myself the target of giving managers something to leave the course with other than just 'more knowledge'. What is more important at this stage is that I have begun the business of creative writing.

PURPOSE

Examining the purpose will help me to refine my goals into workable objectives. It is part of the answer to the question 'Why?'

Let us use the time management example again.

> **The purpose of the course is to help managers make more effective use of their time.**

Not very earth shattering, is it? Nor should it be. That is what I want the course to do. 'Why should I attend?' a manager asks. Back comes the answer from the pages, 'Because you might get some practical help in using your time better'.

We could have presented the introduction and purpose in one section. That is fine – sometimes. However, the statement of purpose should be crisp and clear. On the whole I think that it stands out more powerfully as the final answer to 'why?' on its own.

What about the purpose for our performance appraisal course?

> **The purpose of the course is to improve understanding of the reasons for performance appraisal, the basis of an objective approach, the manager's role, and the problems to be resolved.**

That would give both me and my trainees some idea about what is to be covered. It will help me with the formulation of objectives – the next step.

OBJECTIVES

We need the introduction and purpose statements to identify where we are going, and why we need to go there. We need the objectives to tell us how we will know when we have arrived. The trainees need to know in what way they will be different; or what they will be able to do differently or better. The organization needs to know whether the experience will be, and has been, worthwhile. Getting the objectives right is clearly critical.

I have already mentioned Robert Mager's book where you will find information about how to write good objectives. There are other problems though. As Mager implies, good objectives can sometimes appear rather 'small beans'. To be 'good' you will be able to measure the objective's achievement. That means focusing on one thing at a time. That generally means there are no sweeping claims to achieve

The rationale

greatness. If others read your objectives they may feel they are pretty trivial. For instance, in our appraisal course what could we actually measure?

As a result of the course, participants will:

- be able to understand the reasons for appraisal;
- know the major factors to be included in an appraisal system;
- understand the role of the manager in appraising performance;
- be able to appraise the performance of their subordinates effectively.

Quite frankly, as far as objectives are concerned, that is hogwash (well – perhaps not *entirely* hogwash, but . . .).

What do we look for to determine whether participants *actually understand* the reasons for appraisal? We could get them to list the agreed reasons for appraisal – that would be a start. Then maybe the objectives should be about listing the reasons – that would tell us that they have remembered them.

Still, how would it really help in getting the job done *after* the course? 'Knowing' something sometimes is not much good as an objective either. It is not *action* orientated. If someone knows something, that does not mean that they can or will apply the knowledge. They could list the factors to be included.

The same applies to the 'role of the manager' objective listed above. If they understood it, would it mean that they could, or would be able or willing to carry out the role?

As for the last objective in the list – we would need more than two days to find out whether they might be able to 'appraise the performance of their subordinates effectively'. And other factors beyond this course would have a strong influence, for example their basic managerial competence and their existing skills and potential before joining the course.

The 'objectives' listed do have two functions though. They give me, the writer, an idea about what I will put in the course, and how I will structure it. They also give my clients – the people who asked me to do this in the first place – some indication of what the course will look like. And it *looks* reasonably substantial. My clients would probably accept them because that is what they would normally see, and because it is a reflection of their original request. For those reasons we may have to couch our 'published objectives' in those terms. (Remember, for whom else are you writing?) However, for the person who has to design, develop and deliver the training, they are not really good enough.

In fact those objectives are more like goals, and as such are quite useful. We can either leave them as they are in the outline (and write better session objectives when we get down to write the text), or we can take a longer view. We can go back to the original brief and figure out what they will have to *do* with the information and practice the course will provide them with.

As a result of the course, participants will have:

- agreed with managers and colleagues the problems of the current appraisal system;

- agreed the factors to be included in a new system, and developed an action plan about how that will be carried out;
- an action plan to identify their subordinates' performance appraisal training needs;
- identified their own further training needs.

My objectives are about the action outcomes of the course, rather than the learning that might take place during the course. There may be a strong case also to specify the skills and knowledge that trainees will acquire during the course. However, for now, and for the purpose of this book, I will stick to my action outcomes only.

Now I have some clues as to how I will structure the course. I know I am going to have to get the participants and their subordinate managers together to do something before the course. I have to cover the 'factors' in a way that participants understand, and are prepared to 'run with'. I have to develop some kind of experience (exercises?) that shows a system in action so that they can judge what sort of further training might be needed for themselves and their subordinates.

The format of the rationale has encouraged me to think through more carefully about the *results* that my clients are looking for. If I am wrong they will tell me when they read through my outline, or just the rationale. All in all I feel that it is not a bad start.

Let us try some objectives for the time management course.

As a result of the course, participants will have:

- identified the three most wasteful 'time wasters' in their own job;
- developed an action plan to eliminate them.

Within one week participants will have discussed the action plan with their immediate manager, and decided the actions and timeframes for improvement.

That may seem a little modest, but it is achievable; it answers the brief, and it is measurable. We will be able to find out whether the course has 'worked' or not. What does it tell me about what I will have to do?

There will have to be some pre-work so that participants can identify their time wasters according to a common format. (We will need that to be able to deal with these during the course.)

We are going to concentrate on only three 'time wasters' for each participant. That should give us plenty of time to talk about them. We can then really explore whether they have it in their own power to resolve the problems.

When they have finalized their 'big three', they are going to have to commit themselves to doing something about them. They are also going to need to engage the help of their own immediate manager. That means we are going to have to take into account the practical realities of their work situation.

Participants' managers or nominators are going to have to do something too.

That means they will have to get some information about the course – and their role in it – before the event.

As an aside you will have noticed I am big on action plans, and might seem less concerned with training or learning objectives. Actually, I want to know that someone has or has not done something with a learning experience rather than whether they *know* what they could do. This may not be appropriate for all situations.

APPROACH

Now to the final part of the rationale, the approach. This is where I commit myself to the style or 'feel' of the experience that I am designing. I have already decided that both of the courses I have mentioned will be of short duration, with a down-to-earth, practical style. Pre-work seems appropriate for both. (I do not like people turning up to a course with a 'do something to me' attitude. Pre-work is one way of reducing that possibility. It also saves time on the course itself.)

I think I can use the same statement of 'approach' for both courses.

> **Participants will need to complete some simple pre-course tasks. This will allow a focus on their own work realities. The course will be practical rather than theory-bound, and will have an action orientation.**

I think that is enough. (I might add just a little to the appraisal course.) If my experience is anything to go by it will be attractive to the organization's leaders who increasingly have 'bottom-line' preoccupations. My brief is clearly a 'do something now', not for a long-term development process.

To summarize

The rationale has taken quite some time to complete. While it is one of the shortest elements of the manual, it is also the toughest to write. Making sure you are in tune with your brief is of vital importance. Getting your objectives right can be really tough. You may also need to try out a few ideas, and discuss them (with clients, potential trainees, other trainers) before you complete this.

The actual writing may take only an hour or so. It could take longer. It is worth the effort. It is important to start out in the right direction.

You might want to play around with a few ideas (for exercises, content, and so on) before completing the outline, or indeed the rationale. You might need to do that before you finalize your objectives. It does not matter where you start, as long as when you have finished, you have actually finished everything.

However, the rationale sets up your manual – the one you are writing. You will find that investing time here will be more than worth the effort.

Let us see what the work I have done so far looks like when it is all put together. Let us see how it 'talks to us' – how it shows us what else to do in the outline. After you have read the two examples which follow I think it would be a good idea for you to take a break from reading and practise a little.

Take a course that you have already written, or one you are working on now, and prepare a rationale for it. Does it help you to think a little differently about course design? If it does not I have messed up a bit, or you are already doing good work, or . . . .

PERFORMANCE APPRAISAL

Duration: Two days

For: Senior managers

Introduction:

Performance appraisal is worth covering in any programme of management development. There are two main reasons. First, an organization's success depends on how well its employees do their work. Someone has to make judgements about that. The more disciplined and accurate those judgements are, the better the feedback and corrective action will be. Second, the activity of appraising performance can be conflict-ridden. Even if it were easy to understand it would still be difficult to do well.

Purpose:

The purpose of the course is to improve understanding of the reasons for performance appraisal, the basis of an objective approach, the manager's role, and the problems to be resolved.

Objectives

As a result of the course, participants will have:

- discussed with managers and colleagues and reached agreement about the problems of the current appraisal system;
- agreed the factors to be included in a new system, and developed an action plan about how that will be carried out;
- an action plan to identify their subordinates' training needs;
- identified their own further training needs.

Approach:

Participants will need to complete some simple pre-course tasks. This will allow a focus on their work realities. This course will be practical rather than theory-bound, and will have an action orientation. The course will provide participants with the information and ideas needed to help improve the company's appraisal system.

The rationale

TIME MANAGEMENT

Duration: Two days

For: Managers in all areas

Introduction:

A manager 'manages' many things: people, situations, resources. Always among the scarcest of resources is time. Without managing that properly everything else becomes more difficult. This course will provide some practical actions that managers can take to make sure their time is used as productively as possible.

Purpose:

The purpose of the course is to help managers make more effective use of their time.

Objectives:

As a result of the course, participants will have:

- identified the three most wasteful 'time wasters' in their own job;
- developed an action plan to eliminate them.

Within one week participants will have discussed the action plan with their immediate manager, and decided the actions and timeframes for improvement.

Approach:

Participants will need to complete some simple pre-course tasks. This will allow a focus on their own work realities. The course will be practical rather than theory-bound, and will have an action orientation.

A LITTLE MORE

These examples are of the common or garden variety. The basic model. That will be enough for the majority of courses you will write. Sometimes it is not. Sometimes we need slightly to modify things: expand the introduction or purpose because the topic is new, or controversial: give the approach special treatment.

Let us see how the format was used for a different sort of course – an activity that was part of a major organization development exercise.

This rationale is from one of a series of seminars (part of a process of changing organizational culture) conducted at various levels in the organization. The basic task of the seminar was to inform people about what was happening, gain commitment from them, and involve line management in the delivery.

You will notice a number of differences. Line managers already had some experience of this seminar. They had been through the process in a previous 'higher level' seminar. It was thought that with a little help from the purpose statement, an introduction was not needed.

'For' and 'duration' were changed around simply because in the organization in which it was used it was thought to work better that way.

'Purpose' is lengthier than usual. It substitutes a little for not having an introduction. Besides that, some weeks had passed since the line managers' first experience. It was a way of reminding and focusing them on the nature of the continuing exercise. It outlined and reminded them of the content of the seminar.

Objectives were not set. Direction and end results were relatively open ended. The information to be passed and the participative processes to be used were the important things. It was not directly about performance improvement. It was to presage change and begin 'recruiting converts' to it: part of an ongoing process with many other component parts, all contributing to the planned end results. (I neither defend nor denigrate this choice. There were expectations of specific outcomes, they were not written in this document. *I* think it would have been a useful exercise to have specific objectives for this course, but it was neither my game, nor my rules.)

There had to be more in the approach than usual. It was as much a comfort-giving job for line manager deliverers as it was an information exercise.

This expanded format seemed to work well. See what you think. When you have finished reading the example, maybe it is time for a little more reflection and practice before moving on to the next chapter.

QUALITY CUSTOMER SERVICE

Third Level Seminar

For: All managers and supervisors

Duration: One day

Purpose:

The purpose of the seminar is to:

- help raise awareness of quality customer service (QCS) work in the company and their potential contribution to it;
- show how the company's mission statement, service and management strategies relate to working practices;
- help develop a set of 'best practices' which will form part of their day-to-day work;
- allow managers and supervisors to define the impact of QCS on their leadership, and to make an input to the shape and future direction of QCS in the company.

The rationale

Aims:

The aims of the seminar are to:

- create an awareness of quality customer service;
- create an awareness that managers and supervisors will lead and ultimately benefit from quality customer service;
- provide a structure for managers and supervisors to demonstrate behaviours which will help achieve the company's philosophies;
- create commitment among managers and supervisors to quality customer service;
- create an awareness of 'what is going on and what is happening' in the promotion of quality customer service in the company;
- help everyone understand that the company is *one* team working together towards a single goal – to be the best at satisfying its customers in the market place.

Approach:

The seminar is to be a quality experience using quality materials. A line manager's guide (to run the seminar) and all participant materials will be produced by the Training Department.

The scene will be set at the venue with posters and wall charts based on the contents of and outputs from previous seminars. These will be produced by the QCS team.

The seminar will contain a mixture of session inputs, information sharing and syndicate work. Video tapes will also be used to reinforce the principles of quality customer service.

The skills and experience of the line manager will be drawn on to emphasize points made during input sessions.

The line manager's participation in the previous level seminar will enable him or her to understand and support the experience his or her own group are now going through, and help to alleviate any concerns which may arise.

The line manager will be expected to listen to participant views and encourage open discussion among the group. Their support for the group is critical to the success of the seminar. It will also establish a higher level of trust and support which will be transferred to their day-to-day working relationships.

Most importantly, the line manager's role is to help provide the environment in which the participants will become motivated to participate and learn. This motivation needs to be maintained back on the job so that the learning and enthusiasm is transferred to their work environment, and more importantly, their staff.

A member of the QCS team will help manage the process of discussions and syndicate work, to support the line manager and enable him or her to concentrate on the content of the discussion.

Material and outcomes from all preceding seminars will be used. In this way a comprehensive view of organization thinking can be developed.

4 Content summary

Now we have finished the really hard part we will move on to writing the content summary. You will find that this is where your writing will pick up a little pace.

FLY ON THE WALL

It is really important to get a feel for your task here. Think of it as writing a story (again, for someone else to read). As you are writing it, occasionally close your eyes and visualize what will be happening. See yourself as a fly on the wall of the training room watching you work. What do you see? What do you hear? How does it feel?

Get into the dynamics of the thing. This is a living experience you are describing. You will have done these things before: working with syndicate groups, debriefing a film, talking through an overhead, drawing discussion from the group, walking around the room, checking back to your manual. Visualize these as you write your content summary. Think about the theme music.

While you are writing make some side notes about time and timing. Let your mind (and pen or keyboard) flow. Get your ideas down quickly. When you've written your first draft, review it. Think of the syndicate exercises you want to try. Draft them. See how they might work. Check to see how you need to change the content summary you've written.

Visualize your 'group discussions'. How will you achieve the desired outcomes? Have you described that well enough in your content summary? You will probably find yourself writing some material twice or maybe more. You are committing your thoughts, your course design work to paper. It is a good way to test them out before you try them on your trainees.

HOW MUCH TO WRITE?

How much or how little information should you put in? Well, remember you are 'writing for someone else'. You have to write enough to make sure that there is a clear indication of content, process and pacing.

I once read a content summary for a five-day course written on two pages. Wow! The economy of words was matched only by a similar economy of ideas. It did not give me a clue as to *how* the content would be dealt with. I could not judge how each section contributed to the results we were looking for. The writer had put in the 'what' ('In this section we will cover the importance of . . .') but not the 'how'. I certainly would not have written the same course as the original writer.

I could not. What is more, I had no confidence that the writer had any real idea at this stage about the dynamics of the course; how it would unfold, develop, achieve objectives. We were virtually back to 'discuss motivation with the group'. The writer wanted to get on with the job (good), and did not want to be bothered with a lot of planning (not good).

Two things concern me about that. The first is that in the business of training *process* is vitally important. Consider the almost ridiculous content of some of the exercises we inflict on our trainees. Who could imagine the usefulness – in practical terms – of having people argue in the comfort of a training room about what they would take with them after they have crashed in the desert? It *has* to be the process that is important. The outline I mentioned gave no clues about process.

The second concern is that trainers can leave too much room to make things up as the course goes along.

It is not that trainers do not care much for their performance. It is more to do with getting so wrapped up in a course, and our own sense of 'knowing all' that we can lose touch with what is happening to our poor trainees! It is almost as if they become only an adjunct to our work, not the reason for it.

Of course, a completed manual would ease my concerns, but more thought needs to go into the planning stage. Discussions about a course can be more focused then. Changes are easier to manage. It helps to keep us learner-focused rather than trainer-focused. The content summary must have enough substance to give a clear indication of process.

THE PERFORMANCE APPRAISAL EXAMPLE

Let us work through some examples of writing the content summary. I will start with the performance appraisal course. I am keeping that one-page rationale in front of me, closing my eyes, and visualizing what I think it will be like.

Getting started is sometimes a problem. You need some sort of design outline beyond your rationale. There are many ways to approach course design. One of these is to make a 'mind map' of what I think the whole programme will look like. For simplicity's sake I will use this approach in this book and an example is given in Figure 4.1.

Furthermore, before I continue: while I am writing this quick first draft of the outline other thought processes are at work; other things will occur to me. The outline will begin to talk back to me, and tell me other things I will have to do. I will comment on these at the end of each session outline.

Ideas like this occur in the real situation. It is best to work with some notepaper alongside your outline. Note ideas, questions, possible exercises, visuals, films,

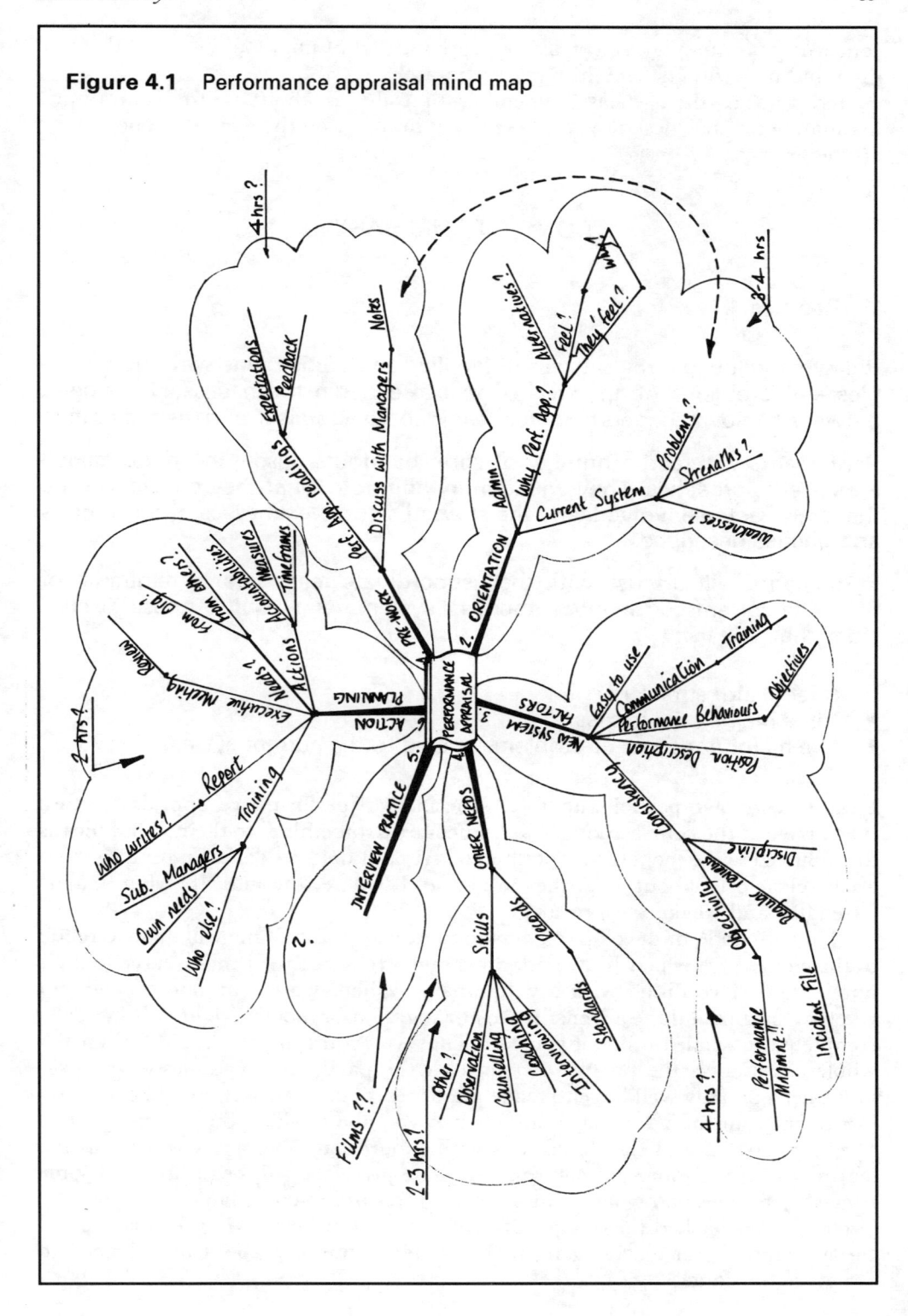

Content summary

Figure 4.1 Performance appraisal mind map

concerns (and time), and so on as you work through. I might add some of these to my mind map, others I might record separately.

Here we go, then. Please remember that this is about writing a training manual, not course design work. Do not get hung up on the content, concentrate on the process.

CONTENT SUMMARY

1 Pre-work

Pre-work will begin the process of familiarizing participants with the principles and problems of appraisal. It will also begin the necessary dialogue between senior managers and their teams about appraisal, and their roles in it.

Participants will read a number of short handouts describing performance appraisal approaches. They will identify and note what they consider to be the major factors involved, and the strengths and weaknesses of the various approaches described.

Participants will discuss with their subordinate managers (a minimum of four) the current performance appraisal system. As a result of these discussions they will list:

- three major strengths;
- three major weaknesses;
- five major concerns or problems related to the current system.

I want to involve participants in this business of performance appraisal before they arrive at the course asking that 'someone do something' to them. That means that I have to give them plenty of time to carry out the pre-work. I must also write a very clear brief about what they are to do. I will need to indicate what 'major' (strengths and weaknesses) means.

I have to 'find', or develop some handouts on appraisal. One will have to relate to the current system. If I have not done much research yet I might have to do it now, before I continue with my summary. Whether I do or not depends on whether the ink and the adrenalin are flowing. If your mood is right, it is better to complete the whole outline if you can. That way you can get a rapid feel for the whole experience; the balance between all the parts; the dynamics of the programme. You may well have to make major revisions later, but it will be worth it just to get your material chattering back to you about what you have to do.

The handouts and the discussions with subordinate managers will begin the learning process before the course starts. The pre-work will begin to build some necessary bridges and generate support for the work to come later.

How I approached the design task does not matter here. What does is to show the guidance I am receiving from the content summary about how I need to structure the course.

2 Course orientation

This session will focus on the reasons for an organization using a performance appraisal system and how the current system seems to operate.

Participants will 'brainstorm' on the reasons why an organization chooses to use a performance appraisal system. The list generated will be discussed and priorities agreed. The consequences of not using such a system will be explored.

Participants will break into two groups where they will discuss one of two questions:

- How do *they* (the senior managers) *feel* about their performance being appraised?
- How do they think their subordinates feel about performance appraisal?

The two groups will reconvene to discuss their results. It is important to determine whether the participants themselves have negative feelings about appraisal, regardless of what they initially agree. Assumptions about how others feel will also be examined. Differences between the two group outputs will be explored. Finally, why people feel (or are assumed to feel) as they do will be discussed.

Agreements will be recorded on flipcharts and displayed on the wall of the training room.

Participants will be divided into three syndicates to share the outcome of their discussions with their subordinate managers. They will compile a list of strengths, weaknesses and problems in each syndicate. Differences between individual's results will be explored.

When reconvened, a final list will be agreed. This will be recorded on flipcharts and/displayed on the wall. The list will be reviewed against the results of the previous discussions.

My mind map indicates that my course will run for between 12 and 16 hours. I will not know exactly how long until I have finished the whole manual. At that time I will know whether I have to add to or trim material, or whether I might have to put more work into pre-work. I might have to negotiate for more days, or . . ..
    This will become clearer as I continue to write the content summary.
    All course administration details, and the settling down process will be taken care of in 'orientation'. I know that, you know that. I leave it out in the content summary.
    I have an initial concern about seeing this as one session. On a rewrite I might put the second exercise into its own session ('current system'). Why? The way it is now, it does not give me enough feel for pace or logical build up. When I explain the structure of the course to participants (as I surely will) they will want to know when they can talk about their pre-work. It will become obvious if I separate out

the two parts. They will not be preoccupied wondering about it. They will be more likely to concentrate on the matter in hand.

My opening work will seek to legitimize performance appraisal as an organizational need. If I do not deal with that how can I expect motivated learning and subsequent action?

I have talked about 'negative feelings' that may not come out. These are senior managers I am working with. They will have a sense of loyalty to the organization that may prevent them opening up, and expressing any negative feelings they may have. If I do not do something about that I cannot adequately service the needs of the total (not just training) exercise. My content summary reminds me that I have to deal with it.

I have already decided to decorate the training room with flipcharts because we will need them when we get to the really important part – action planning.

Two final comments here. I mentioned earlier about a overly vague content summary. Had this been done in the way that gives me the horrors, all that would have appeared in 'orientation' would have been the first paragraph. I have written only a couple of hundred words more, but I have shown something of the 'how' of what I intend to do. I have also reminded myself of several important aspects that have to be considered when finalizing the course and the manual. I have not got bogged down in detail.

And – you will see I have put a couple of syndicate exercises in the orientation session. Most are relatively easy to understand – by trainers, that is. If, however, there is anything unusual, or out of the ordinary about the content or process of an exercise you are thinking about, write about it in the content summary, where you (or someone reading it) can judge the impact and meaning quickly.

3 Performance appraisal factors

This session is intended quickly to focus on the more positive aspects of a future system rather than the problems with the current approach.

Participants will discuss the performance appraisal systems studied in their pre-work. They will discuss their perceptions of the structure, content, strengths and weaknesses of the various systems one by one. Key comments will be recorded.

In syndicates, participants will agree the basic factors to be included in any system.

Debrief will:

- list the factors;
- expand on how factors are to be covered;
- determine which of these are present in the current system, which seem to work/not work, and why.

Participants will compile a final list of factors to be included. As before factors will be listed on flipcharts and displayed on the training room wall.

Content summary

This session will be the major effort in creating a better understanding of performance appraisal and what lies behind it. My mind map reminds me of the salient points I want to make. The job will be to draw them out from the group. That means extensive discussion of the pre-work examples. I have left myself some room to determine how much time I am going to spend here. This will depend on the total balance when the manual is completed.

4 Other 'system' needs

A Performance Appraisal system is more than the forms to be used. It must be supported by behaviours and skills. This session is designed to determine what those 'extra' supports are.

Participants will view a film about performance appraisal. They will then agree the main points. Discussion will include what is thought to be 'missing' from the film.

Participants will then work in syndicates to identify 'other needs'.

As each need is identified a brief description of the need, and how it applies will also be agreed.

Debrief will develop a final list (and descriptions) of needs. The level of difficulty of satisfying these needs in the organization will be discussed. As this discussion takes place all previous work recorded will be reviewed for its continuing relevance. Agreed points will be recorded and added to those already displayed.

At the conclusion of this session it should become obvious that for performance appraisal to be successful a 'higher' system must be implemented – that of performance management.

I have not chosen a film yet. I am going to have to review some. It need not matter if the film's contents are at odds with previous discussions. As much can be made of difference as of similarity.

You will see that I have not included all the information in my mind map in this (and the previous) session. That will be recorded later, when writing the detail.

My content summary reminds me that we are going to cover not just the 'what' of appraisal, but also the 'how' and 'why'. It also reminds me that there will be plenty of flipcharts on the walls of the training room. I had better make sure the facilities will allow it.

The bit about performance management occurred to me as I was writing the summary. It is not specifically asked for in the original brief, but I did not want my participants (the senior managers and designers of a new system) to think that once the 'forms had been put right' everything else would naturally come out better. (Anyway, performance appraisal systems are doomed to fail unless they are part of a larger performance management system. If I did not move towards creating that understanding I would not be answering the organization's needs – only its wants.)

The mind map, and the session on 'Other Needs' has persuaded me that I ought to cover the wider issue. It will help in action planning. The act of writing quickly – just covering my main thoughts about what is going in the course has provoked other ideas. We will see how these work out when writing the detail.

One more thing occurred to me when writing this part of the outline. I was going to try to put some work in on the appraisal interview. (After all, most films about appraisal will cover it, if not concentrate mainly on it.) Once again, a feel for the balance and pace of the course tells me I should deal with this separately.

It will take some time to cover, even briefly. 'Skilling up' is not one of my objectives, so I could leave it out. Still, if I can cover it, even briefly, it will add to the strength of action planning, particularly when it comes to identifying further training needs.

Being 'reminded' or 'persuaded' often occurs when writing the content summary as quickly as you can. Let ideas flow, occasionally close your eyes, imagine the process. Quickly read what you have written and assimilate that feel for pace and balance – and of course, listen to the theme music.

5 Appraisal interviews

An interview is one of the cornerstones of a performance appraisal system. It is the time and place real damage can be done; to manager-subordinate relationships, pride, motivation, subsequent performance, and the organization's credibility. This session will explore the importance of the interview. It will reinforce the importance of 'other needs' and of effective performance management.

Participants will discuss the requirements of an appraisal interview. They will 'build' a 'model' to be followed. (All previous work will be taken into account.)

Participants will then be divided into three groups. They will be given case studies and role play briefs. Each syndicate will prepare one interview as interviewer, and one as interviewee. Part of this preparation will include agreement of expectations of process and outcomes. One from each syndicate will be nominated to role play later the interviewer and one the interviewee.

Groups will agree the problems to be raised/managed during the role play.

At the conclusion of preparation, role plays will take place. They will be observed and noted (as per brief provided) by all not taking part in the role play itself. As each role play concludes, expectations and what actually happened will be discussed. The role plays will be videotaped as an aid to debriefing.

Final discussions will build on earlier conclusions about the requirements of an appraisal interview.

Well, I have let myself in for plenty of design work here. I am going to have to write case studies for role plays, role play briefs, observers' briefs and, of course,

I am going to have to describe how people are to prepare. I am going to have to validate the process for the participants. There's not enough time for everyone to practise, so who is going to get picked on and why?

My objective in doing this has more to do with making sure the participants know how tough things can be, and may be more prepared to look closely at themselves and their training needs, rather than ignore the problems and difficulties, or blame them on something else. (We all have a way, from time to time, of recognizing problems – everywhere but within ourselves!)

I am not sure that I have written enough about how this practice session will run. It could have been worse. I could have described it merely as 'syndicate exercises, preparing for, and role playing appraisal interviewer, interviewee'. I may have to test market this part of the content summary before I go much further. (Would any two of us write the same sort of syndicate briefing? If you closed your eyes and visualized events, would you be watching the same activity as I?)

I am going to have to arrange for a video camera on the day.

This session is going to take quite a bit of time to work through. I may have to trim some of the earlier material, or this, or ... At any rate, what I have written seems to me to reflect what I was imagining about the process and dynamics. My outline is still talking to me.

6 Action planning

This session will translate the information and discussions of earlier sessions into plans of action for each of the participants.

The course will be reviewed, mainly by reference to the material noted on flipcharts and displayed on the walls of the training room.

The group will discuss and agree a format to be used when formulating action plans.

Individual participants will then consider and note:

- actions that they will each need to take, with information relating to timeframes, measures of progress and success, help needed from others;
- actions others in the organization need to take.

It will be important to focus participants on what they can do themselves rather than 'delegate the responsibility' to others in the organization, or the organization at large. Participants should also identify their own training needs and potential actions to meet these.

Participants will then review their action plans in pairs.

Action plans will then be discussed with the whole group, to refine them, and to determine where they should, and can operate together in the senior manager group.

During action planning the course facilitator will assist participants to formulate their plans.

Once again I have not covered all the information in my mind map in the content summary for this session. There will be room for that in the detail of the manual.

I am going to have to think through some ideas about how action plans will be drafted. I will have to provide substantial process help during this session. My outline reminds me that participants may want to spend their time action planning for others (not on this course). This will need careful attention. They may well sew the seeds of their own failure by creating action plans for others that they can neither control nor encourage or persuade others to carry out.

I have indicated that participants should identify their own training needs. Our objectives certainly include that. However, participants may well need to review their own needs after the course, when they complete an analysis of their own subordinates' training needs.

Right – I have finished the content summary. To see if you can get a better feel for balance, logic, pace, dynamics – and the theme music, in what follows I have reproduced the whole summary together. I have modified the 'orientation' session. See how you think it works.

CONTENT SUMMARY

1 Pre-work

Pre-work will begin the process of familiarization of the principles and problems of appraisal. It will also begin the necessary dialogue between senior managers and their teams about appraisal, and their roles in it.

Participants will read a number of short handouts describing performance appraisal approaches. They will identify and note what they consider to be the major factors involved, and the strengths and weaknesses of the various approaches described.

Participants will discuss with their subordinate managers (a minimum of four) the current performance appraisal system. As a result of these discussions they will list:

- three major strengths;
- three major weaknesses;
- five major concerns or problems related to the current system.

2 Course orientation

This session will focus on the reasons for an organization using a performance appraisal system.

Participants will 'brainstorm' the reasons. The list generated will be discussed and priorities agreed. The consequences of not using such a system will be explored.

Participants will break into two groups where they will discuss one of two questions:

- How do *they* (the senior managers) *feel* about their performance being appraised?
- How do they think their subordinates feel about performance appraisal?

The two groups will reconvene to discuss their results. It is important to determine whether the participants themselves have negative feelings about appraisal, regardless of what they initially agree. Assumptions about how others feel will also be examined. Differences between the two group outputs will be explored. Why people feel (or are assumed to feel) as they do will be discussed.

Agreements will be recorded on flipcharts and displayed on the wall of the training room.

3 The current system

This session will concentrate on that part of pre-work concerned with discussing with subordinate managers the present performance appraisal system. It should focus on both positive and negative factors.

Participants will be divided into three syndicates to share the outcome of their discussions with their subordinate managers. They will compile a final list of strengths, weaknesses and problems in each syndicate. Differences between individual and syndicate results will be explored.

When reconvened a final list will be agreed. This will be recorded on flipcharts and displayed on the wall. The list will be reviewed against the results of the previous discussions.

4 Performance appraisal factors

This session is intended quickly to focus on the more positive aspects of a future system rather than problems with the current approach.

Participants will discuss the performance appraisal systems studied in their pre-work. They will discuss their perceptions of the structure, content, strengths and weaknesses of the various systems, one by one. Key comments will be recorded.

In syndicates, participants will agree the basic factors to be included in any system.

Debrief will:

- list the factors;
- expand on how factors are to be covered;
- determine which of these factors are present in the current system, which seem to work/not work, and why.

Participants will compile a final list of factors to be included. As before the list of factors will be recorded, and displayed on the training room wall.

5 Other 'system' needs

A performance appraisal system is more than the forms to be used. It must be supported by behaviours and skills. This session is designed to determine what those 'extra' supports are.

Participants will view a film about performance appraisal. They will then agree the main points. Dicussion will include what is thought to be 'missing' from the film.

Participants will then work in syndicates to identify 'other needs'.

As each need is identified a brief description of the need, and how it applies will also be agreed.

Debrief will develop a final list (and descriptions) of needs. The level of difficulty of satisfying these needs in the organization will be discussed. As this discussion takes place all previous work recorded will be reviewed for its continuing relevance. Agreed points will be recorded and added to those already displayed.

At the conclusion of this session it should become obvious that for performance appraisal to be successful a ('higher') system must be implemented – that of performance management.

6 Appraisal interviews

An interview is one of the cornerstones of a performance appraisal system. It is the time and place real damage can be done; to manager–subordinate relationships, pride, motivation, subsequent performance, and the organization's credibility. This session will explore the importance of the interview. It will reinforce the importance of 'other needs' and of effective performance management.

Participants will discuss the requirements of an appraisal interview. They will 'build' a model to be followed. (All previous work will be taken into account.)

Participants will then be divided into three groups. They will be given case studies and role play briefs. Each syndicate will prepare one interview as interviewer, and one as interviewee. Part of this preparation will include agreement of expectations of process and outcomes. One from each syndicate will be nominated to later role play interviewer and one, interviewee.

Groups will agree the problems to be raised/managed during the role play.

At the conclusion of preparation, role plays will take place. They will be observed and noted (as per brief provided) by all not taking part in the role play itself. As each role play concludes, expectations, and what actually happened, will be discussed. The role plays will be video taped as an aid to debriefing.

Final discussions will build on earlier conclusions of the requirements of an appraisal interview.

6   Action planning

This session will translate the information and discussions of earlier sessions into plans of action for each of the participants.

The course will be reviewed, mainly by reference to the material noted on flipcharts and displayed on the walls of the training room.

The group will discuss and agree a format to be used when formulating action plans.

Individual participants will then consider and note:

- actions that they will need to take individually, with information relating to timeframes, measures of progress and success, help needed from others;
- actions others in the organization need to take.

It will be important to focus participants on what they can do themselves rather than 'delegate the responsibility' to others in the organization, or the organization at large. Participants should also identify their own training needs and potential actions to meet these.

Participants will then review their action plans in pairs.

Action plans will then be discussed with the whole group, to refine them, and to determine where they should, and can operate together within the senior manager group.

During action planning the course facilitator will assist participants to formulate their plans.

To summarize

Well, there it is. There is nothing unique and mysterious involved. It is simply a matter of quickly visualizing what needs to happen and writing sufficient to ensure that your memory will not falter when you write the actual detail.

If you have read it through with your imagination open you will have a feeling for how *you* would write up this course, and, of course, how you would run it. At this point we would have recognized that in two days there is little time for skilling our senior managers. We would have recognized that there is still some work to do to achieve the objectives. We will now be able to write the detail in such a way as to 'manage' this situation.

So far we have not spent much time writing. If, when the detail is being written, the session does not seem to be one that will work out, we can modify our original ideas without having wasted very much effort. If we need to rewrite one of the sessions, we can immediately judge whether something else will need to change. Writing the content summary in such a way gives us a relatively permanent helicopter view. When something changes, we can still see the whole picture and the balance in it.

During the process of writing the content summary it is likely that we would have had to 'step aside' for a while and write something else; a syndicate exercise, for instance. We might do this to give a better idea of time and timing, or to try out a different idea for tackling something. Since there is no great body of detail to get lost in, popping in and out of writing the content summary is not difficult.

The format so far has not involved any extra work. One way or another you will have to cover the same ground when writing up a course. The style of this approach – and particularly the content summary – helps with the design work considerably.

We also have a document that we can take to our 'masters' to check how closely it matches *their* perceptions of need. Although we will not have spent much time on it we will have a fairly detailed description (with what is written, and what is still lodged in our mind's eye) of the whole course. We will be able to answer the 'what if' questions.

We can also take the content summary to our customers – the senior managers – and ask them what they think. We can step outside the job of course design for a short while, take on board some more ideas and perhaps tighter direction, and then return to the job again – and the flow is still there.

If we were going to use our rationale for publicity purposes (as part of a brochure for instance) we would use the titles of the content summary. In this case I would change them a little. Perhaps as follows:

Preparation
Why performance appraisal?
The current system
Performance appraisal factors for success
Other needs
The appraisal interview
Action planning

In my course summary I have used titles that are useful to me as guides to writing the manual rather than publicizing the course. Still – there is nothing to stop me changing my content summary titles to these if they help me better to visualize how the course should go.

Two more examples follow. As usual, they include my comments. If you think you have seen enough of how to write the content summary, skip past them. You can always check back later. Maybe you would like to take a stab at writing a content summary for the time management course. My mind map is on page 49. Work from that. Or you could try one of your own. You decide.

Content summary

THE QUALITY CUSTOMER SERVICE EXAMPLE

Let us cover some of the work of the quality customer service course. One of the sessions is called 'Yes buts'. The major inputs of the course have been made, and it is time for the participants to look to themselves for their contribution. A second session follows. It is about overcoming the 'Yes buts'.

7 Yes buts

Participants will discuss the barriers to their implementing quality customer service initiatives in their own areas.

8 How will problems be solved?

This session covers the service improvement process, listening to our customers, standards of operation, and effective management practices.

I am only kidding! This is the way it might have been written. It says 'what', but it certainly gives no indication of 'how'. There is no feel for time, or dynamics. There is no theme music playing. It has that old economy of words and ideas. It is pedestrian. It is inadequate. I do not want to have to wade through the detail of the manual to find out what is going to happen. This is the way it was really written.

7 Yes buts

At this stage of the seminar there may be issues which participants feel will act as barriers to implementing QCS in their own areas. This session is designed to bring these issues into the open, and have the group determine how *they* will deal with them.

In syndicates participants will decide what will get in the way of implementing quality customer service. These things are often identified as 'labels' only. ('staff numbers', 'head office', for instance.) Debrief will clarify and describe the issues to ensure complete understanding. Issues will then be placed in priority order ready for action planning later in the workshop.

The combined list, in priority order will be noted on flipcharts, and displayed.

(Effective management practices, to be covered in the following session, will also contribute to action planning.)

8 How will problems be solved?

This session covers the service improvement process, listening to our customers, standards of operation and effective management practices.

An overview of each of these initiatives will be given by the line manager. Participants will be invited to question how these initiatives will contribute to overcoming barriers, and make their jobs easier. They will explore their specific role in implementation. During this discussion reference will be made to the discussions and outcomes of previous workshops.

The prime focus of this session is developing effective management practices (EMPs). (These are the agreed commitments to minimum service standards based on the company's 'values'.)

In syndicates, participants will develop their own EMPs, using their line manager's EMPs as examples and focusing on the company's values. Each value must be considered separately. Actionable, measurable statements of intent will be developed from them which will demonstrate participants' commitment to service-orientated behaviours. (These can be followed-up and supported by the line manager.)

When syndicates return to the main room, EMPs will be discussed and agreed. They will be noted on flipcharts and displayed for later reference and inclusion in action plans.

Finally the group will develop individual and group/team action plans based on all previous work, agreements and decisions.

Better, isn't it?

TIME MANAGEMENT EXAMPLE

I have sketched out a mind map from the time management course (see Figure 4.2). They are my first thoughts about the course, so I may make substantial changes when I actually write the content summary and see how it all feels.

As usual, I want some pre-work done. (I think it is an important way of pointing people in the right direction before a course.) The session after the introduction will cover the pre-work. It will compare what people have read, noted and experienced, in relation to their jobs. The next session will show some new material in a film (not yet chosen), and compare that with all other 'information' participants have. (I want to show as many ways of managing time as there will be reasons for not doing it, because 'this doesn't fit my circumstances'.)

It is in this session that I want to turn attention to what participants can actually do. It is where I will build some commitment to improvement. I am then going to run some form of case study. I do not know what yet, but I figure it will be the time to do some heavy road testing on participants' understanding of the subject. I will develop a fairly substantial exercise for the group and/or individuals. Until the case study/exercise is designed I cannot complete my course outline. I intend to get on with it and finish what I can quickly.

My final session is the action planning session.

The introduction, time wasters and managing time sessions will take up the first day. The case study and action plan sessions, the second.

Content summary 49

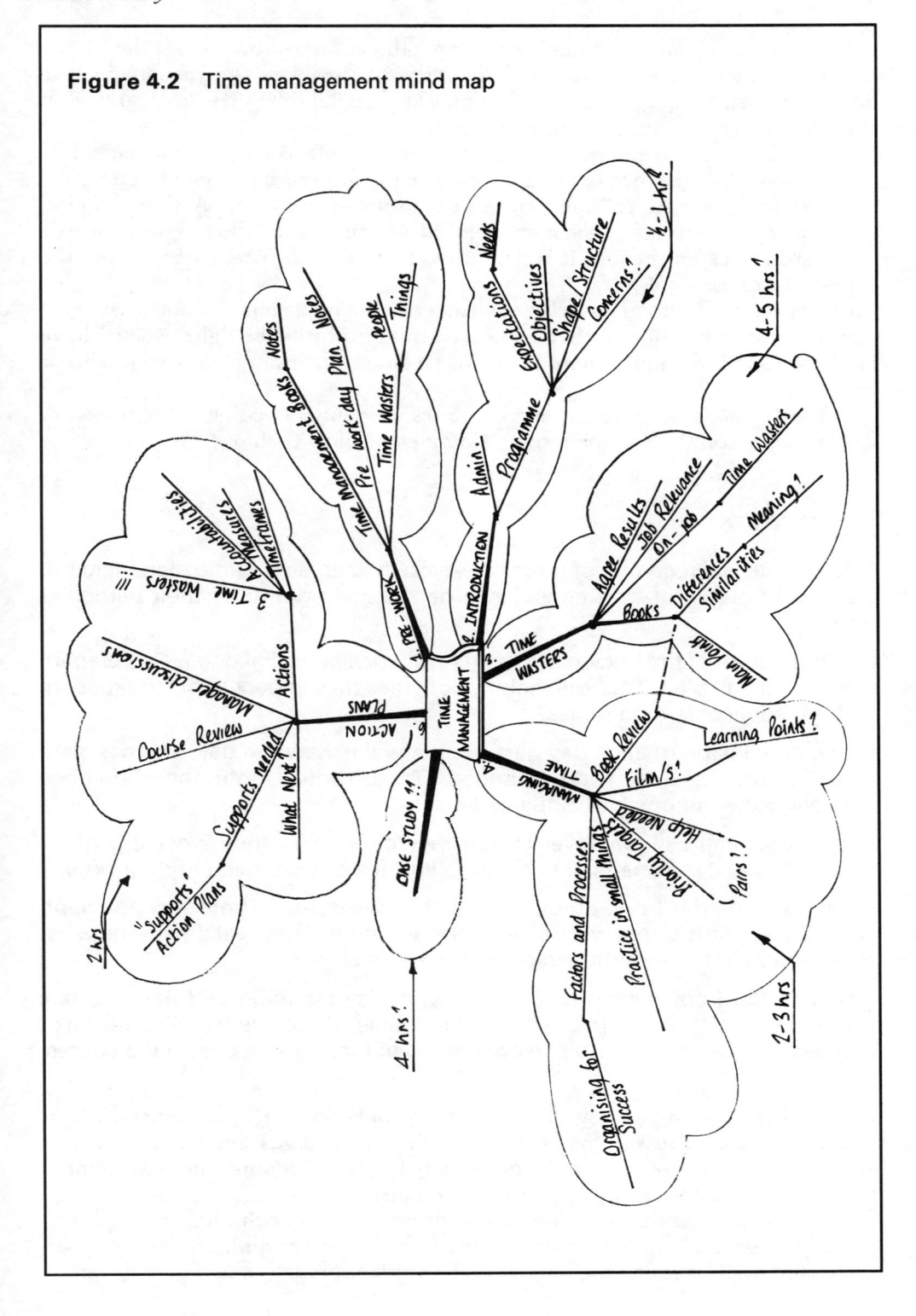

Figure 4.2 Time management mind map

Let me remind you about the objectives for this course – how modest they are. I am making no claims about how well all participants will be able to manage their time after it. All I am aiming for is that they know what time they 'lose', and why; and then to do something about it themselves.

Of course I want them to understand the fundamentals of time management. If they do not, they will not have much chance for success, but my only interest is that they understand it enough to be able to improve on the job. Action planning will show me that. If they need more help then I can give it; either in the course or afterwards, back on the job. It is then up to them and their managers to put the experience to use.

Of course it is up to me to sell the virtues of time management, and I will give that my best shot. Still – if they are not 'turning towards the light' when I have finished, there is not much more I can do, except maybe examine my own skills or lack of them!

OK. Let's go. I am going to write two sessions only. The first is the pre-work session, the second – managing time. Comments follow each one.

1 Pre-work

Participants will read one of three books on the subject of time management. They will note what they consider to be the main points of their particular book.

On completion of the book participants will, for a period of one week, prepare a pre-work day plan. This will include activities they expect to be engaged in, and the applicable timeframes.

At the conclusion of each day participants will review the day, and compare actual events against those planned. They should note the difference between expectations and actual events.

Participants can use whatever format they choose for their work day planning. (Clearly it is beneficial to try to follow the advice given in their book.)

As a result of the book study, and of the week long 'time management' experience, participants will consider the situation. They will determine what appear to be their own three biggest time wasters.

Notes on the book's main points, pre-work day planning and time wasters should be sent to the trainer prior to the course. Conclusions will be formed and used – in a general, not personal or individual sense – during the course.

I have to get at least four copies each of three books on time management. I have to specify the format that 'notes' must take in participants' pre-work. I have to allow time for the pre-work to be done, noted by participants, and sent to me. I have to plan time to 'analyse' participants' notes.

It will be interesting to see how different books guide, help, or hinder participants. The group will be better prepared to learn (about both a learning experience, and applying it on the job). The pre-work approach should give the group some confidence in its self-sufficiency and the ability to take more control of time and events.

My analysis of participants' notes must include my perceptions of what their experiences and views seem to mean. This will give me background information to use during discussions.

I am going to have to read the three books!

The 'time wasters' session will be about four or five hours long. As the mind map shows, we will discuss the books and explore what they might mean to participants. I might put a syndicate exercise in there.

I will check on how people feel about what they have read, and how it has job relevance – and deal with the consequences of their answers.

I will look at time wasters (expecting differences between people and situations) and see if we can decide cause, effect and potential responses.

Why not take a break from reading and make a stab at writing the summary for the 'time wasters' session. When you have finished that, see if there is a balance in the three sessions – including the one I am about to write now, 'managing time'.

4 Managing time

The session will move participants from an understanding of the 'structure' of time management to that of the process and supports needed.

Participants will view a film. They will discuss the major points made in the film and compare these with the points made in the set books.

In syndicates, participants will discuss the factors, actions and processes important to effective time management. For example, good organizing skills, respect for the use of others' time, saying 'no' when it is required, diary disciplines, and so on. (The facilitator will need to help the syndicate process along to ensure participants understand what they need to do.)

Views of what has to be taken into account, what has to be done, and how it must be done will be noted on flipcharts for whole group discussion. Final agreements will be noted and displayed on the training room walls for reference during action planning.

Participants will then work in pairs to determine what they personally believe are the facilities needed to support good time management. (They might decide time diaries, secretarial services, pagers, and so on.) They will agree the priority needs and an outline 'benefits statement' that can ultimately be used with their managers to enlist their help.

Well – I have to find a good film for the group. I have to view it, study the support documentation and compare that with the books provided. I will have to 'analyse' similarities and differences. I will take a 'position' *vis-à-vis* this analysis and the notes (of pre-work) sent by participants.

I am going to have to come up with a *comprehensive* explanation of 'factors and processes'. I am going to have to get some examples of diaries, 'time diaries', or 'time manager logs' (etc., etc.), for people to examine. I should not have any trouble getting companies to donate these. They will see a potential sales opportunity.

I am not going to let syndicates struggle through their work unaided – trying to guess what it is *I* want. I will be working with them, trying to help them verbalize what *they* see as factors and processes.

Although not as often as people state, factors outside of our control often upset our time management plans. Other people and things outside personal control need to be managed somehow. It is likely that our participants will need some help and support (from those other 'people and things') to improve their own time management abilities. I may have to help them put their 'arguments for assistance' together. Will I need to do a 'mini-teach' on something like cost benefit analysis? I had better have something ready . . . .

While working on this session I decided that the 'practice in small things' should go to the case study session, as an introduction. (By that I mean that participants should practise on the easier aspects of time management, and develop their skills, before tackling the harder aspects of the work.)

I have also decided to add something of a review. I am going to ask participants at the end of day one to think overnight about our use of time. I will look for comments at the beginning of day two. It will give me some clues about what is sticking in their memories. It will help me to run the case study in the directions participants need.

I will leave you to write the rest – the case study and the two final sessions if you want to. Maybe you can make use of it?

That is all for the content summary. Let us move on.

5   Timetable and lists

This chapter covers the last two sections of the outline of the manual, the timetable and lists. Though each of these sections are straightforward and simple, their value should not be underestimated. They too have an important part to play.

TIMETABLE

There are at least three versions of timetable in common usage. One is a straightforward list of times, such as:

```
Day 1
 9.00 –  9.10    Introduction and Admin
 9.10 – 10.15    Discuss Pre-work
10.15 – 10.30    Morning Break
```

and so on.

Another is the boxed diagram, an example of which is shown in Figure 5.1. Either of these can be used for 'publicity', showing participants in advance or at the beginning of a course what is going to happen when. The timetable I am concerned with serves a different purpose.

After reading through the content summary (in preparation for running the course), the timetable gives an accurate picture of *pace*. It can add significantly to the understanding of how the course is supposed to work.

It is a working document used in two stages – when you are getting ready to run the course, and during the course itself. During preparation it serves as a quick reminder of the handouts, visuals, films, and so on that you will need, *and* when you will need them. During the course a quick glance (totally unnoticed by participants because you are so good at this), will tell you how you are doing for time, what the overall impact on time gained or lost will be, when the next visual or handout is due, and so on.

Figure 5.1 Example of a 'boxed' timetable

		Day 1	Day 2
a.m.	8.30	Introduction Admin Principles of fibbing Jargonology and numbers Divide and confuse	Statistics case study preparation Case study
p.m.	1.00	Economics and truth Intro to statistics Methods More on fibbing	Case study
	5.30	Review of stats Prepare for Day 2	Case study debrief

The construction of the timetable serves as a reminder of what comes next, and as a 'running' summary of the whole course.

When you look at the timetable in Figure 5.2. It is a document to be occasionally glanced at, but a full and powerful reference should you need it. It is from a course I ran a long time ago, and I have modified some of the information for this presentation.

Let me explain the column headings first. They are, from left to right:

T   What page of text is it?

V/HO   Is there a visual or handout here?

(untitled) What is the page of text called?

Mins   How many minutes will it take to work through this page of text?

End time   When it ends, what time will it be?

Notes   Is there anything else I need to know? Is there anything else I want to write here?

I will explain what a page of text is when I elaborate on writing the detail. The 'T' number merely identifies it. There are only two kinds of pages in the detail; text and copies of visuals. They are similarly numbered. The numbering system ensures that you cannot lose a page (unless you really try, of course).

'V' show whether there is a visual (overhead transparency or any prepared visual aid) with this page of text. The number relates to the corresponding page of text and is not the number of visuals there are. This helps in preparation – making sure your visuals are properly arranged and located in the right place in your delivery. It is a matter of debate as to whether it is more or less confusing to have your last of ten visuals numbered 24, or having mentally to juggle with T10, V4; T15, V6, and so on. I obviously believe it less confusing to number visuals according to where they are used, not how many there are.

'HO' identifies whether a handout, or 'other piece of paper' is distributed during the delivery of the material in the page of text numbered. It includes the 'normal' information extracts, syndicate exercise briefs, case study briefs, role plays, and so on. Once again there is a signal to you, both in preparation and in actual delivery, that it is 'time to give out paper'.

The untitled section, for the titles you give to your pages of text, is for the labels you stick on the material contained in each page of text. Clearly these labels represent yet another quick summary of what is going on.

The next section is as it appears. It shows how long – in minutes – you plan for this material to take in its delivery. Avoid saying 'It depends on the group.' Your planning should attempt to take these variations into account. And remember, it is a plan; a statement of intent. Realities will modify times and the timetable is designed to 'capture' these time fluctuations.

'End time' is the clock time expected when the material is expected to finish. Trainers need to keep a fix on time. It is one of the things to be managed in the

Figure 5.2 Preferred timetable

T	V/HO		mins	end time	notes
		Programme start		9.00	
1	1	Introduction. Objectives	15	9.15	
2		Approach	10	9.25	
3	3 HO	Role of the supervisor	15	9.40	
4		Leadership	15	9.55	
		Break	15	10.10	
5	5	Leadership – basic style – 1	15		
6		– 2			
7		– 3		10.25	
8	8	Effectiveness	15	10.40	
9	9	Assessing the situation	10	10.50	
10	HO	Leadership exercise	70	12.00	Brief 10 Task 30 Debrief 30
		Lunch break	60	1.00	
11	11 HO	Motivation Maslow – 1	20		
12		Maslow – 2		1.20	
13	13	Herzberg	10	1.30	
		Syndicate exercise	60	2.30	Brief 5 Task 25 Debrief 30
14	14	Expectancy and perception	30	3.00	
		Break	15	3.15	
15		Groups – Introduction	10	3.25	
16		Syndicate exercise	60	4.25	
17		Review day 1 – Close	35	5.00	

training room. The timetable removes some of the problems of getting lost in the experience, and losing that important control.

The notes section can carry any information. I have shown, for example, the time breakdown I have planned for syndicate exercises. 'Brief', 'task', 'debrief' means 'set up and explain, do the job, talk about it afterwards'. It can be used to put other reminder notes in, for example, where a film is to be shown. The notes section should also be used by the trainer to record, in pencil, important time variations as they occur. If something actually takes 50 rather than 15 minutes, record it. It should be part of your own review, and preparation for the next time you run the course – or similar material. You need to review the difference between your design and what actually happened. Similarly, record other events of interest which will fit in with the quick, holistic review of the course a timetable provides.

You can get a different perspective of your course when checking your timetable. If it does not look right; if it does not seem to have a sense of logic, then maybe you need to change something.

As I said, you cannot complete the timetable until you have written the detail, but it belongs here initially to help with your preparation for running a course.

Take another look at the example I have used. Close your eyes (*after* you have looked at it!). Can you see this course unfolding? Does it give you a feel for the process such that you can support or argue with the flow, or with time spent, or ...?

LISTS

This is the final section in the course outline and is just what it says. It is the reference page for everything else you have in your manual that you should find in support documentation. There are lists under the titles of:

- Visuals
- Handouts
- Syndicate exercises
- Case studies
- Role plays
- Participant information – for example:
    pre-work brief/s
    joining instructions
    course schedule
    etc.

However, the first item in the lists is the list of facilities you will need to run your course.

Facilities/equipment needed

- one training room
- three syndicate rooms

- five flipchart boards
- chart paper
- felt pens (charts)
- whiteboard
- felt pens (whiteboard)
- participant name cards
- participant folders, writing paper, pens
- overhead projector and screen
- bluetac
- video camera, recorder, monitor
- 16mm film projector
- films – 'The Appraisal Interview', 'Conflict and You'.

Once again, it is part of the preparation for a successful course. The check lists (if you use them) will make sure you do not have to go running out of the training room to pick up something you have forgotten. It will also save a lot of time and discussion if you are among the unfortunate trainers who are not able to organize things for themselves, and someone else has to do it for them.

CHECKING BACK

That is all there is of the course outline section of the training manual.

Remember, it is made up of a number of components, each providing a different type of summary of the course, the main one being the content summary. A couple of hours to write, a few minutes to read, it holds the main session headings, with just enough detail to give you a real feel for the content, process and dynamics of the course. It tells you the 'how', as well as the 'what' of the course.

Before we move on, just for the hell of it, see if you can write down all the various components of the course outline – in the right order. To write this sort of manual effectively, and quickly, it is important to know the structure well. It should automatically come to mind. If it does not, you will struggle somewhat, and you will be less inclined to stick to the format.

When you have finished, check back to diagram 2.3 and the brief explanation. How did you do? Can you now move on with confidence to writing the detail?

6 Writing the detail

This is where most of the work is done. It is also where most objections arise concerning a standard format:

'The training room is not a place for a script.'

'Trainers will not use the same words every time they run a course – it is impossible.'

'It is too much trouble, and absolutely unnecessary.'

I will give a qualified 'yes' to the first two, an unqualified 'rubbish' to the third. Let me explain. Writing the detailed delivery notes *is* very much like writing a script. That is well in line with the need to introduce interest and drama into your work. However that is only one small reason for doing it. There are others.

The first relates to the old 'discuss motivation' or 'cover the following main points' problem. There are always specific ideas, key words and phrases, which must be used in all training material. Writing the detail, or 'text' as it is called, wraps up these key ideas in comprehensible English (or any other language in which you are writing). The total sense or meaning can be conveyed (to the trainer, the person to whom the text speaks first) when this approach is used. It leaves far less room for questions of 'how' or 'why'.

The second reason is that the format or process gives a good idea of pace and timing. Writing and reading through your text can give you reasonably accurate indications of the amount of time you will need to cover all of your material. It can also help ensure you have the right structure in your course. You have a better idea about this when you review what is being delivered or 'spoken'.

My final point has to do with development of the material. I have already strongly advocated the need to visualize the experience you are planning – down to the last detail. Writing the text as fully as I suggest will be a reasonably fair reflection of that visualization process. And it is not as rigid as it might first appear.

The text is written to include your key ideas, words and phrases in *the kind of way* you might say or deliver them. They will be your first or preferred choice. This is the way you can see yourself doing it. On the day it is highly unlikely that it will be the exact way you will deal with your material. Many things will intervene. Your memory, the circumstances you face at the moment you face them, other ideas that occur to you, the needs of your trainees.

The important point is that you have written them, that you have them to fall back on, especially in those very rare moments when your mind goes blank. (I know that it *never* happens, but if it should, imagine the comfort of a prompter at your side.)

On the day you're almost certain to say much more (sometimes a little less) than is actually written. What you say, how you hear it, what your trainees do by way of response/no response will lead you into drawing on that infinitely greater-than-you-have-written knowledge. And you will know – because you have your text and timetable at your side – that those on the spot modifications and embellishments are right, rather than rambling.

For all of the reasons I have mentioned, stick with it. Reasons should become even clearer in the last section which deals with how actually to use the manual in action.

A brief consideration here, though: the manual structure is based on the premise that when you have finished writing it, you will hardly need it. It becomes a sort of reference to be turned to when you can afford the time to glance down to check if what you wanted to do has been done, and to check what you're going to do next.

THE FORMAT

The format virtually guarantees that you will not be note dependent. The outcome of the process, the finished manual, provides the right kind of safety net for running a course. For this reason the symbols used, the use of space, layout, and so on, are important because of the almost subliminal messages they offer about the 'what', 'why' and 'how' questions.

After discussing some of the 'why do it', I will cover some guidelines about 'how to do it'. Remember, I am proposing the following information as 'guidelines', not rules to be followed. Still, I think it would be better to see the guidelines as essentially firm. Do not ignore them until you have given them some real hard testing under fire. (Persist before you desist.) I have found the process works well and to deliver what I need in the training room.

The individual parts of the pages of the text will not make much sense as only individual parts. They have to be seen as a whole. The structure is designed to give the mind other messages when your eye flicks ever so briefly over the page during occasional moments of your delivery. (By the way, you might like to write in your objectives for each main section of your detail. This will help to keep you focused when you are delivering.)

I will start by outlining the guidelines, and where necessary giving a brief explanation. When I have finished that, I will show a double-page example which will serve as a summary. (You will see what I mean in a minute.)

The detailed text is actually two pages. The right-hand page contains the text. The opposite, left-hand page contains a copy of any visual to be shown, where there is one.

The *left-hand, facing page* is where your copy of the appropriate Visual goes. *There should be no more than one visual to each page of text*. That's for ease of operation. When you turn your page it is important that you immediately see everything that you are going to have to deal with. If there is more than one visual, it becomes confusing trying to sort out what comes first, second, and so on.

You should only deal with one idea on each page of text, and the visual is more or less a summary of that idea. If that means that your page of text doesn't *have* much text in it, so be it. Your eye picks up an immediate message from large areas of space on a page, and in this case that may be: 'there is nothing much to say'.

Some pages of text will not need the support of a visual. (This is especially so when it takes more than one page to deal with 'an idea', as it does more often than not.) If there is no visual associated with a particular page of text, the opposite ('facing') page can be used for highlighting key points, individual trainer notes, ideas for how a whiteboard or flipchart might look when the trainer 'builds' a diagram out of discussions with the group. It can be used for anything the trainer running the course wants. Alternatively it can be left blank.

You might not want to put a title on each of the visuals you will actually use, but you should title your copies. It is good for your lists, and it will be used in your text page.

I generally think of my visuals as overhead transparencies. Of course you can use slides or prepared charts, or anything you please. I think of it in this way because it is an easy shorthand. Besides that, though, I think assaulting the senses of trainees with a variety of forms of visuals should be questioned. Of course there may be times when such variety is needed, but it may be little more than a self-indulgent need of the trainer to impress the trainees that drives such a decision. At any rate there is the possibility that a 'variety light show' will serve only to confuse. It is also more difficult for the trainer to handle, so think carefully about it. Indulge me a while longer.

I was once training some managers, and dealing with 'change'. I would work out this fantastic chart I was going to draw while delivering a particular piece of information. It was going to be a chart (with its x and y axes) showing the exponential rate of growth of change. It was to have a couple of embellishments. When it was completed I was going to turn it upside down and – lo and behold – it would be a picture of a dinosaur, and it would make my point perfectly.

Well – I did it, and I impressed me enormously. Unfortunately, the only message that I got across to my trainees was that I was a bit of a twit.

The right-hand page is slightly more complicated. Only slightly though. The page has three sections: a top section containing page (text) number in the top right-hand corner, and title of the information the page covers – where you can see them immediately you turn to it; a left-hand column, about four centimetres wide with your 'delivery instructions'; a right-hand column – the bulk of the page – where you write your detailed notes.

In the left-hand column (the delivery instructions) there are a number of symbols which point to what you should be doing at any given time. These can be recognized at a glance, they do not need reading. They stand out when you scan the page in that microsecond glance you take when checking where you are and what you have to do next. Some of these symbols are written in lower case, because it is more of a *suggestion* to follow, some in capital letters, to indicate that it is more of an instruction to follow.

In the right-hand column there is text (what you say – more or less) and trainer notes (what you are supposed to do – more or less). It is important to differentiate clearly between these two areas. For this reason I normally write (type) text in upper case and trainer notes in lower case. The briefest of glances (normally all you have time for when delivering) will tell you whether these are words you say or instructions you follow. It is easy to see the difference.

Research shows that words are easier to read when printed in lower case, but reading is not the problem. You do not really read these notes when you are delivering: you glance from time to time at the key words and phrases 'wrapped up' in your text. Upper case letters are normally bigger and I have found them to 'present' better – to be easier to spot. If you have access to desktop publishing you may want to experiment with different fonts and different size of fonts – whatever makes it easier to absorb both instructions and information rapidly as you need to.

The symbols and brief explanations are shown below.

text	THIS IS WHAT YOU WANT TO SAY (MORE OR LESS) IN THE WAY YOU WANT TO SAY IT (MORE OR LESS). GIVEN THAT YOU'RE LIKELY TO 'USE' MORE WORDS IN THE ACTUAL EXPERIENCE, TEXT IS A KIND OF LENGTHY SUMMARY OF WHAT YOU SAY. THE FULLER, THE BETTER.
note	This is what you do, and/or cover, or get others – your trainees – to do. It is also used when what you want to say has a little more flexibility or ambiguity than your text can handle. (You will see what I mean in the examples given later.)
V	Show your visual now.
HO	Distribute your handout now.
FILM	Show your film now.
VID	Show your video now.
WARNING	This is a 'watch out' signal. The trainer must pay attention to accompanying notes *before* the session begins. (This symbol is rare used, and is mainly a back up for the unfortunate trainer who hasn't had the time to prepare properly in advance of the course beginning.)

I have so far said that the right-hand column had only text and notes. That is a bit of a fib. It has a lot of space and spaces too and this is also used to give messages to

Writing the detail

the eye and mind. The way space is used on a page can be quite helpful, and it should be used as carefully as words and sentences.

When writing the course outline an objective discussed was that of getting material to talk back to you; to ask you things, to tell you things. Well, the format of the detail is the same. It is designed to talk to you all the time you are running the course. And just as it is in normal conversation, meaning is conveyed by much more than words.

To know just how much information is passed by the symbols and patterns used in the process, try the squint test. This is something I discovered to have value for me. Look at a page of text, close your eyes until the detail of what is written disappears into greys and white – little more than a blurred pattern. What information does that pattern give you? 'There are things I must say here, trainer notes tell me I must do something differently; I will be putting on a visual (half way down the page), I will need to get a handout ready', and so on.

It seems to me that the squint test gives about the same information as you might pick up out of the corner of your eyes, or in that tiny glance you take at the material in front of you. Yes, I know it is a bit funny, but it can work with practice, if you let it.

Pages 64–5 show a pictorial representation of what I have just described. They will be followed on pages 66–7 by a general example – a first page of text covering some administration details before a course really gets under way. **Read through these pages before continuing**.

Well, there it is. Yes, of course it is all a little old hat. I could have written the whole thing in the ('note') section, but I wanted to show a more or less full layout, text and all. Under normal circumstances the page would more likely have been all trainer note with a visual and a handout breaking it into three parts.

For instance a trainer note might have said:

note   Welcome participants.

                Cover admin arrangements such as:

                Rooms' layout
                Toilets
                Tea/coffee making facilities
                Course schedule
                Lunch times – more rigid
                Fire precautions (ensure people know procedure and exits)
                Cover self-introductions and expectations of the course. . . .

In fact that is more like the way experienced trainers would probably do it, given that it is straightforward standard material. It would save on paper and it is also simpler to deal with, to work with.

When to use text or trainer note is not an easy decision to make. It depends on a number of conditions, including the amount of space on the page you have, whether you want to avoid splitting up an idea over two or more pages, the simplicity/complexity of the idea or material you have to cover, or the potential

VISUAL TITLE (e.g. 'symbols')

text	What to say
note	What to do
V	Put on visual now
HO	Issue handout now
FILM	Show film now
VID	Show video now
WARNING	Pay attention to this before going on

Writing the detail

T number

TITLE OF THIS PAGE OF TEXT

WARNING	A last minute preparation device. For instance: 'You should study the visual before moving on'.
text	THIS IS WHAT YOU SAY (MORE OR LESS). IT WRAPS UP YOUR KEY WORDS AND PHRASES IN EASY TO UNDERSTAND LANGUAGE. YOU NEED TO REMEMBER TO USE SPACE AS WELL AS WORDS HERE.
note	This is where you give yourself a little more freedom. You give yourself some instructions, say when or how, or how long to run a syndicate exercise. You might want to list some main points you wish to make during a discussion with participants. You can list them here if there is no room available on a blank facing (opposite) page.
V	Show your visual. The title goes here.
HO	Issue your handout. Again, the title goes here.
FILM	Show your film. Same thing with the title.
VIDEO	Show your video. Ditto.

V1 LAYOUT OF TRAINING CENTRE

Writing the detail   67

1

INTRODUCTION AND ADMINISTRATION

text	WELCOME TO THE BLAH BLAH BLAH PROGRAMME.
	JUST BEFORE WE KICK OFF I'D LIKE TO COVER JUST A FEW ADMIN DETAILS.
	THIS IS A NEW BUILDING FOR ALL OF US SO I GUESS THAT I'D BETTER MAKE SURE YOU KNOW WHERE THE IMPORTANT ROOMS ARE.
V	Layout of centre
note	Go through visual showing facilities, rooms we will be using. Make sure everyone knows where exits are and what to do in the case of a fire.
text	OK I'D LIKE QUICKLY TO COVER THE SORT OF SCHEDULE WE'LL BE WORKING TO THIS WEEK. THE TIMES ARE MORE OR LESS APPROXIMATE. HOW LONG THINGS WILL TAKE WILL DEPEND ON YOU MORE THAN STICKING TO THE TIMETABLE.
	ONLY ONE FINAL THING THOUGH – WE NEED TO STICK TO THE LUNCH TIMES. WE'LL GET A REVOLUTION IN THE KITCHEN IF WE DON'T!
HO	Outline schedule
note	Work quickly through the course schedule. Clear any questions before moving on.
text	NOW I KNOW SOME OF US KNOW EACH OTHER, BUT NOT EVERYONE. I THINK IT'S IMPORTANT THAT WHEN WE WORK THROUGH THIS COURSE WE KNOW WHERE EVERYONE IS COMING FROM. SO I'D LIKE PEOPLE TO INTRODUCE THEMSELVES AND SAY WHAT THEY THINK THEY MIGHT GET OUT OF THIS COURSE.
	SO YOU KNOW HOW MUCH OR HOW LITTLE TO SAY – I'LL KICK OFF.
note	Introduce yourself covering: • name • job/job title • time in the company • highlights of experience • before that • any highlights • expectations of the course Make sure you keep the description to under three minutes.

ambiguity of the material. A reasonable guiding principle is that if you have key words, phrases or ideas that must be delivered, write 'text'.

However you cannot write everything in text. (Well it is possible, but . . .). If you did you would have a manual for a two-day course that would be about a metre and a half thick! For instance, I have found that a page entirely filled with text alone (with no accompanying visual) would take between one or two minutes to work through – if you do not embellish or add to it.

Some of the later examples will clarify this further. Your own experience will polish off the job. How much to write, and in what form, is a matter for common sense, keeping in mind the intentions of the format.

What I will do now is write a few pages of text. There will be three examples. For familiarity's sake, one relates to our performance appraisal course and is the main example (see pages 80–87), and one relates to the quality customer service course (see pages 75–77). For variety's sake one is a completely new example (see pages 70–71). As usual, I will be making some comments after each example. Do not be concerned with content. The examples illustrate the process only.

There is then a final rewrite of each example. To give you some options about how you want to deal with these, they appear as Appendices A, B and C. (Your options? Read these when you are ready for them, or later, as you have the need. If you need no more examples – you need not bother to read them at all). Each of these rewrites have comments added. I suggest that you read the example. As you do, make your own notes on how you might make improvements. Compare your notes with my comments. Obviously there will be differences. Ask yourself why. Work with the material.

If you really want to see how the examples were rewritten right away, then turn to the appendix. If you can wait, read on: refer to the final rewrites later when you have had time to reflect on the examples, your notes and my comments. Ask yourself again why there are differences between what I have written and how you might write the text. You will consider, no doubt, that some differences will be 'more OK than others'.

THE PRESENTATION TECHNIQUES EXAMPLE

The first example is from a short input into a management course. (Trainees had to make presentations during the course, and this session was a 'mini-teach', a quick input so that participants had some sort of standard model to follow.) Again – do not worry about the actual content.

We will start off with the trainer's first attempt to get the ideas down. The example covers the first few minutes of a one hour session. There is one page of text, and one visual in the first attempt. There is plenty of space on the left-hand (facing) page. Use this and whatever other space you can find to note your own thoughts about how the text could have been constructed. (If it is your own book!)

Do not forget, the more finished attempt can be found in Appendix A.

There is no definitive example of the correct way. The writer's ideas about text come from visualization of how things ought to go. You will visualize things differently. That is OK. With no content summary to work from there are bound

Writing the detail

to be some big differences in how to tackle the session. You will probably have some ideas to improve it further. If you do, work on them before you check Appendix A.

Clearly this is only a first draft. There is much more work to be done. The first thing to be said is that this does not pass the squint test. A prime reason for this is that there is too much material on the page; the whole one hour session from which this is drawn took up only three pages. It is all right for a first attempt, but not good enough for our finished manual. There has to be a rewrite.

Now I know that I have said that there is no way of knowing how much to write, but there are some rough guidelines I have found to work reasonably well. That is, if we have a one hour session, some visuals to work through, some discussions with trainees, only minor case study work or syndicate exercises – we can expect there to be around six pages of text.

A page of text with a visual takes about five minutes to work fairly quickly through; a page of text with a modicum of group discussion – ten to fifteen minutes. On the other hand, sessions that are 'activity intensive', with work geared to controlling the activities, might take considerably less time to write, as we will see later.

There is too much material on this page. There are three ideas here: a sort of introduction, 'important factors' and 'attitude'. We would gain some advantage by separating them and writing considerably more about each. The three-page rewrite in Appendix A does just that.

All three pages of our trainer's original text carried the same title. That needed improvement. The reader's eye, glancing at the head of the page would not know if it was the first, second or third page of coverage. The page shown in our example could have included 'Introduction' in its title.

We might have included our session objectives at the beginning of this page, either for our own use, or to share with trainees. This would be in a language appropriate to them. If we made more than one page out of this we could put our objectives on a visual. (Mager [*Preparing Instructional Objectives* (1984), Lake Management & Training] claims that if we share our objectives with our trainees we might not have too much more to do! That would make our work easier as well as learning more certain.)

Our trainer has jumped straight into the session without even defining what 'presentations' are. Again, that might be all right. It depends on the group. I would prefer not to take that sort of chance. If you include information you can always choose to leave it out.

The text is not written in spoken English. How many of us use words like 'prior' or 'reputed' when we speak, unless we are trying to impress instead of or as well as express?

When looking for ideas from the group ('a number of important factors to be considered . . .') the trainer should have some examples ready. These can be part a trainer's note or listed on an otherwise blank facing page. It is the trainer's job to milk these ideas from the group (as well as others the group might think of).

We need to shepherd the group in the direction we believe is most productive. I get the impression from what is written – or rather from what is not written, that the trainer is not visualizing strongly enough. I am not convinced that there will be enough control over process and outcomes. You might argue with that, and

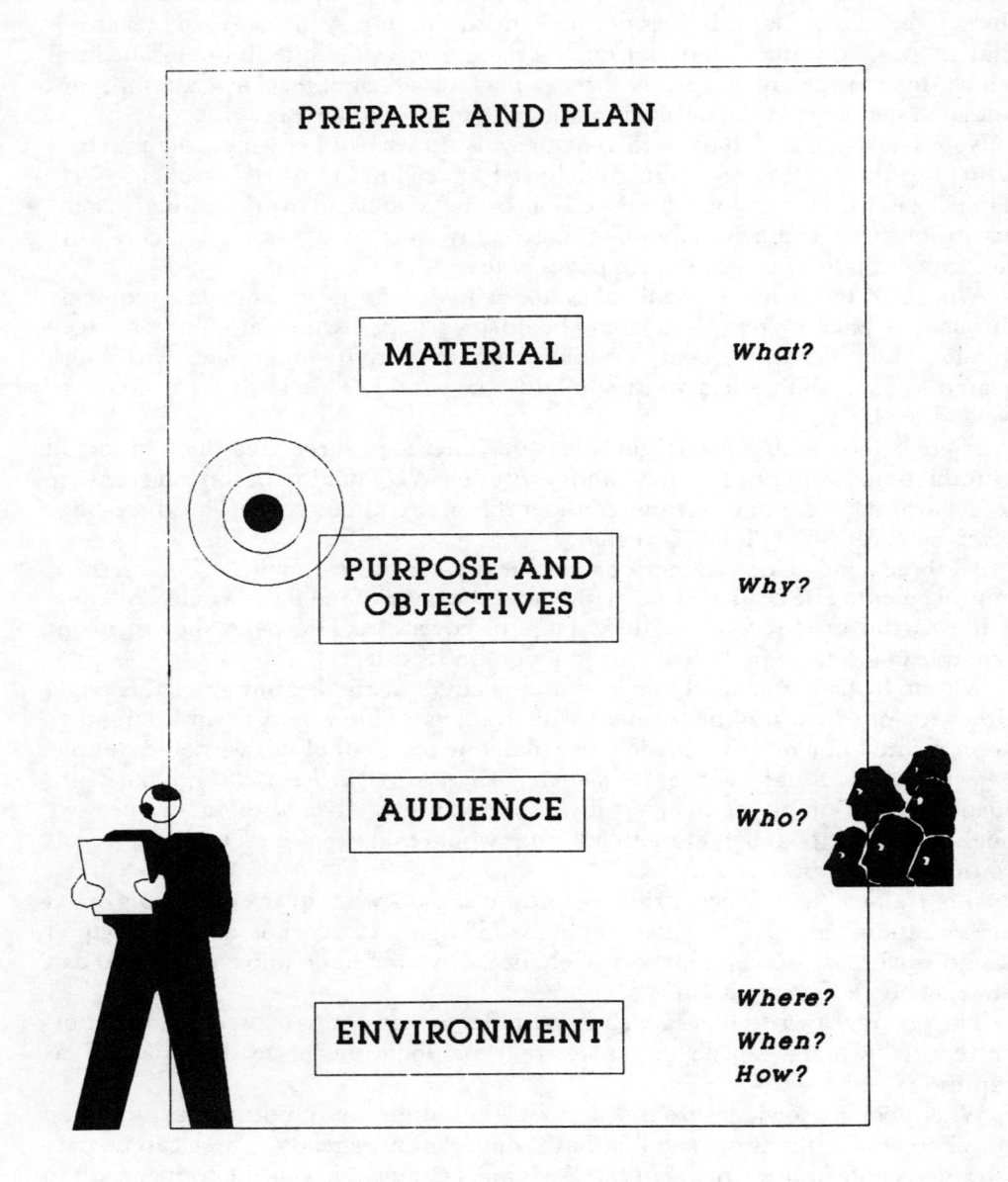

V1

PREPARE AND PLAN

MATERIAL	*What?*
PURPOSE AND OBJECTIVES	*Why?*
AUDIENCE	*Who?*
ENVIRONMENT	*Where?* *When?* *How?*

Writing the detail

PRESENTATION TECHNIQUES   1

text	DURING THE NEXT HOUR WE WILL DISCUSS PRESENTATION TECHNIQUES AND VIEW A FILM ON THE SUBJECT. MOST OF YOU WILL, FROM TIME TO TIME, MAKE PRESENTATIONS EITHER TO YOUR STAFF OR TO CUSTOMERS. CERTAINLY DURING THIS COURSE YOU WILL *ALL* BE MAKING PRESENTATIONS TO THE GROUP, FACILITATORS AND GUESTS. IT IS THEREFORE IMPORTANT THAT WE AS FACILITATORS SET SOME GUIDELINES OF WHAT WE EXPECT THE STRUCTURE OF YOUR PRESENTATIONS TO BE. WITH THIS IN MIND, WE HAVE DEVELOPED THIS SESSION TO SET THESE GUIDELINES FOR YOU TO FOLLOW WHEN PREPARING YOUR PRESENTATIONS. THERE ARE A NUMBER OF IMPORTANT FACTORS TO BE CONSIDERED WHEN MAKING A PRESENTATION WHAT DO YOU THINK THESE MIGHT BE?
note	Trainer to record participants' responses on a flipchart.
text	GOOD. I WILL TRY TO COVER EACH OF THESE POINTS AS I GO THROUGH THE MATERIAL I HAVE PREPARED. THE KEY WORDS ARE PREPARE AND PLAN.
V	Prepare and plan.
note	Any suggestions from the group which can be related to 'prepare and plan' should be ticked on the flipchart list from the previous question.
text	GOOD PREPARATION AND PLANNING ARE CRUCIAL TO GOOD PRESENTATIONS. YOU MUST NOT ONLY PREPARE YOUR MATERIAL YOU MUST PREPARE YOURSELF.
note	Write on whiteboard – 'ATTITUDE OF MIND'.
text	ATTITUDE OF MIND FOR YOURSELF IS IMPORTANT. EVEN THE BEST PRESENTERS GET NERVOUS. IT IS REPUTED THAT BOTH ROBERT MENZIES AND WINSTON CHURCHILL BECAME QUITE ILL WITH NERVES PRIOR TO MAKING PRESENTATIONS. I'M SURE THERE ARE MANY OTHERS TOO INCLUDING MYSELF. BEING NERVOUS IS NORMAL AND NATURAL SO DON'T WORRY – YOU'RE AMONG FRIENDS – DON'T FORGET THEY HAVE TO DO IT TOO! SO THEY'RE ON YOUR SIDE. ATTITUDE OF MIND TOWARDS YOUR AUDIENCE IS IMPORTANT ALSO – TREAT THEM AS INDIVIDUALS AND DON'T TALK DOWN TO THEM. YOUR ATTACK OF NERVES ONLY SHOWS THAT YOU CARE ABOUT YOUR AUDIENCE. IN FACT, LACK OF NERVES MAY BE A DANGER SIGN AND MAY DENOTE AN APATHY TOWARDS EITHER THE GROUP OR THE MATERIAL.

you might be right, but why not put the matter beyond dispute, and not leave it to chance?

What does 'attitude of mind' mean? Will our trainer really use this phrase? I think it is all right for a title, but I wonder whether there is not a better way to say this and get the point across. If it is a key phrase to be used – leave it in. If it is not, leave it out; replace it with something you intend to use.

These are some of the points which occurred to me when first reading this draft. How about you? Remember, when you are ready, Appendix A has a rewrite.

THE QUALITY CUSTOMER SERVICE EXAMPLE

This example is something from our quality customer service seminar. It is the 'Yes buts' session. (Maybe you should take a quick look back at pages 47–52 to refresh your memory).

The session has been preceded by a benefits session called 'What's in it for you?' It will be followed by a session working on how problems will be solved. This session concerns only the barriers to implementing a quality customer service initiative as perceived by the participants. It deals with properly defining the problems, not solving them.

The text shown in the example (pages 75–77) has been preceded by a page describing the purpose of the session and an overview and outline timetable. It is for the line manager's benefit since he or she will be making the most of the inputs. (I would have preferred to have put this and other overviews on facing pages or at the head of the page of text. But – it was not my course, my development work, my department, or my company, so. . . .)

There will not be any problems about the line manager–deliverer understanding the material or handling the tricky aspects of process management. This has been taken care of by quickly working through the manual with the line manager beforehand.

The two pages shown are a first draft. (Yes, it is a real example.) There are no visuals or other pieces of information on facing pages. The line manager has plenty of room to add personal notes. The session is planned to last for one hour (one hour and only two pages). As there are no facing-page visuals for the following two pages of text there are two blank pages for notes.

We should not worry overmuch about some of the 'mystery phrases' in this text. The line manager will have been through this exercise before, as a trainee. The trainer and the line manager would have discussed this session well in advance so that at least *they* both understood the meaning of the terminology used. However, there are a number of improvements we can make before I will feel we have developed a reasonable description of the session.

The changes I would like to make are:

- Improve the titles of the pages so that they 'say' more.
- Put the purpose and overview of the session at the head of text page 21.
- Make a visual of the examples of how issues would be labelled and described.
- Explain the process of labelling and describing better.
- Soften the language – make it more informal and 'spoken'.

Writing the detail 73

- Improve the description of the syndicate exercise and timing.
- Improve the description of how to handle the syndicate debrief and discussion.
- Improve the description of setting priorities or action.

Overall, I find it difficult, even with the content summary, to visualize the process clearly. The improvements are shown in Appendix B. If you can think of other things that would improve this – well done. Perhaps you would like to try, and then compare your work with what follows.

THE PERFORMANCE APPRAISAL EXAMPLE

Here is one last example – from the performance appraisal course, for which we have a full content summary.

There are two complete sessions, 'Course orientation' and 'The current system'. This will be my first draft. When it is done I will make my usual comments, then complete a rewrite of the material. When I have finished all that I will work on the timetable. Both the rewrite and the timetable to which it refers are in Appendix C.

This is the biggest example and it may need a little more concentration and note taking. As you are reading the material (pages 80–87), do your 'eyes closed' thing. Make your own notes for improvement. Compare these with my comments and later, the finished example in Appendix C.

Before I begin writing the text I have to set things up from the content summary. First I have to figure out roughly how long the material might take to work through. My mind map indicates I expect to spend about three or four hours on the sessions. Unfortunately, having an idea of the overall time is not enough. We have to work how this fits in with a number of other factors.

We don't want to have to break off a session or activity part way through just to have lunch – not if we can help it. There should be some sort of natural break when we stop. We are also cursed with the reality that trainees expect lunch to be somewhere in the middle of the day. There might be a revolution if we attempted to break for lunch at four in the afternoon. If our trainees' expectations are not more or less met we will have unhappy, unresponsive people to deal with.

We also need to keep in mind that people do need to take a break every now and again to remain fresh. For these reasons we take custom and practice into account when constructing the course. A break in the morning, one around midday, and one in the afternoon.

How will that fit in with the specific needs of the material, and the training and learning processes? If we can *legitimately* construct our material with this in mind, all well and good. If we cannot, we will know it, and be able to plan how we get around a problem. If we keep it in mind when we start we will not have to 'fiddle' with material and juggle with times when we have all but finished the writing. We will save development time.

I have seen trainers begin the course design process by filling in coffee breaks and lunch times. I absolutely must emphasize that *I am not* advocating the construction of a course around break times. Trainers that do should be drummed

21

YES BUTS

text

AT THIS STAGE OF THE DAY THERE ARE NO DOUBT MANY ISSUES YOU CAN IDENTIFY AS GETTING IN THE WAY OF IMPLEMENTING QUALITY CUSTOMER SERVICE IN YOUR AREA.

AS MENTIONED AT THE BEGINNING OF THE DAY, THIS SESSION WILL BRING THESE ISSUES INTO THE OPEN AND NOT ONLY IDENTIFY THEM BUT LOOK FOR WAYS TO OVERCOME THEM.

note

If appropriate, refer to issues identified so far today on the flipchart at the back of the room.

text

THIS WILL BE DONE IN SYNDICATES. I WANT YOU TO LABEL THE ISSUES AND THEN WRITE 8–10 SHORT STATEMENTS TO DESCRIBE EACH ISSUE. I'LL GIVE SOME EXAMPLES.

note

Facilitator to write the following examples on the whiteboard.

Issue	Description
Staff experience	Staff are too junior/senior No experience in legal/clerical Only ever been in head office
Staffing levels	We do not have enough staff Too many/few supervisors Staff too junior/senior Too much work to do
Type of staff	Recruitment policy wrong Recruitment techniques poor Need too much training

Get the group to help you add other points to the descriptions.

text

PUTTING THESE DESCRIPTIONS AGAINST ISSUES IS A 'SO WHAT' PROCESS. FOR EXAMPLE, WE DON'T HAVE ENOUGH STAFF. SO WHAT? WHAT DOES IT LOOK LIKE, HOW DOES IT FEEL? WHERE DOES IT LEAD? DOES IT SHED LIGHT ON THE SPECIFICS OF AN ISSUE? BY ASKING 'WHY'? OR 'SO WHAT'? WE CAN DECIDE WHETHER THERE IS ONLY ONE, OR MORE ISSUES – HOW THEY MIGHT BE RELATED, AND SO ON.

Writing the detail

22

YES BUTS (CONTD.)

note | Break the group into syndicates. Make sure that the syndicates are balanced in terms of support, personality, positive outlook, and so on.

Each group will need to appoint a spokesperson and scribe to write their issues on a flipchart.

The syndicates will have 30 minutes to label and describe the issues and report back to the large group.

text | THE QUESTION IS 'WHAT IS GOING TO MAKE IT DIFFICULT FOR US TO IMPLEMENT QUALITY CUSTOMER SERVICE PRINCIPLES AND ACTIONS IN OUR AREA?'

WHEN YOU RETURN YOU WILL PUT YOUR FLIPCHARTS UP ON THE WALLS SO THAT EVERYONE CAN READ THEM AND WE WILL COVER THEM IN A LATER SESSION.

note | When the syndicates return and have a 'gallery walk' for 10 minutes, reading the flipcharts from all syndicates, pose the following questions to help prioritize the issues:

- Is the issue the same for everyone?
- If it is the same – can one person working on it solve other problems along the way?
- Where was this issue evidenced more than others?

Once these questions are answered, they can be prioritized, ready for action planning. Make sure it is pointed out that effective management practices may go some way to helping with these issues when we work on them in the next session.

out of the corps. I *am* saying that we cannot be so inward looking to ignore *everything* except the material itself.

We must take into account our customers' needs and expectations. We are not obliged to meet them. We can, by virtue of our communication and selling skills (we have them don't we?) – reshape them. Let us do that with the timetable *if* we have to, but only *if* we have to. We will have enough 'reshaping' to do when it comes to really important stuff like learning.

Taking these factors into account means something like this: a conversation you have with yourself while visualizing what will happen.

> This is what I want to do. How long will it take? An hour and a half or three quarters? Two hours? Where are the natural breaks? If I start at nine o'clock that will mean I won't be starting lunch until around one. Is that OK?
>
> If I start at eight thirty, I can break for lunch around twelve thirty. Is that better? What does that mean for coffee breaks? Can I have one, or will I arrange a constant supply so we can work right through if we need to?

Before I start writing my text I will make some rough notes about *potential* time frames. I will have visualized the delivery of the material, the processes involved, the responses of trainees, and times. I will be all set for success.

OK – I have worked through the content summary. I have made some rough notes about how long each element of the session will take. I have taken into account the natural breaks, and it seems that trainees' expectations about satisfying stomachs, resting brains and stretching legs can be reasonably met. In this case I see the first two sessions taking a morning, with a clear natural break between them. 'Performance appraisal factors' will take up the rest of the afternoon. (There is a lot to cover there, so I will have to have a rethink about that.)

'Other system needs', 'Appraisal interviews', and 'Action planning' will make up a longish second day.

All of day two will be tight. I am going to have to control the first session on that day very carefully. The second session is likely to run on a little. People will be recorded on video. I am going to have to spend some time overcoming shyness or resistance to it. Then no doubt, I am going to have to control the need to justify their actions, defend their 'acting', or just plain talk about themselves when they see themselves on TV!

I'm already short of time for this session. I may need to modify my approach on the day. Fortunately I can eat into the action planning session a little, if needed.

My initial estimate was 12–16 hours. It now seems that it will be closer to the larger number.

Before you begin looking at the next example, why not take another long look at the content summary and mind map for this course? Try to visualize how *you* would run the course. See how that compares with the way I write the detail.

In the example that follows the four pages of text have only one 'real' visual. Two pages have facing pages with detailed information. It should be noted that these are used in quite a different way – as repositories of extra information: checklists, or material that can be read out quite legitimately – such as a syndicate briefing. One word of warning that I might not have heeded myself. Avoid putting too much on facing pages. The information might not 'talk to you' as powerfully as it might.

The example has taken about four hours to write. That includes a couple of breaks to make and drink some coffee, some writers' block, a bit of head scratching, drafting syndicate exercises and visuals. That is about a one-to-one ratio of development time to running time for this part of the course development. Not a bad investment, and in my head I have already run one course (or this part of it).

In looking through my work, I am not too displeased. I have enough confidence in the material to make me feel comfortable about how the course can be controlled. There are a couple of points that could stand a little more thought though.

I have written the administration details in a form of shorthand note only. We repeat this information every time we run a course, so it really does not need any more.

We're in an in-company training situation, participants would be familiar with the facilities and 'ground rules' of the training environment, so it does not require much of an explanation. They know each other. We do not need to go through any participant introductions. I would have spent some time with each one of them during their pre-work, so I do not need to let them know any more about me.

If conditions had been different the administration and introduction would have included appropriately more.

It is clear from the text that a course schedule and a copy of the objectives will be sent out with pre-work instructions. The decision to do that came about when I was writing the material. (That means now, of course.)

I was going to allow about five minutes for the administration section. It may take longer depending on how they feel about the situation, this course, and the work they have to do afterwards. If we take more than five minutes I will have to find time from elsewhere. That is easy. I have two syndicate exercises where I can make time, either by reducing the task time, or reducing discussion time (and making more inputs from the front). I have a coffee break and a lunch break from which I can shave a few minutes. My timetable will give me the 'instant picture'. I will have a better feel when I have finished the rewrite.

In the first page of text I have combined four 'ideas': administration, course schedule, expectations and objectives. Fair enough. These all form part of what one might call an 'introduction'. Still, I am concerned that I might be rushing things. The single page gives me an idea that I am a little over-anxious to get down to work without paying enough attention to any acclimatization process.

I have started in a way that might leave my trainees no opportunity to fidget, take a breath, or get their minds around the experience to come. More pages would force me to take this into account. Two or three pages to replace this one would 'talk to me' in quite a different way.

You will see I have used the break between text pages 2 and 3 to flag up a change of activity. For these two pages of text you will see I use the two facing pages for other notes I will need. I can work directly from these more summary notes and the timetable, without reference to the text, if I want to. My text becomes merely an 'emergency document'. I will look through the detail when participants begin their syndicate work. I can make sure I have missed nothing. If I have, I can plan how to make up the deficiency.

V1

COURSE OBJECTIVES

As a result of this course you will have:

- AGREED WITH YOUR SUBORDINATE MANAGERS AND YOUR COLLEAGUES HERE, THE PROBLEMS OF THE CURRENT PERFORMANCE APPRAISAL SYSTEM.

- AGREED WHAT NEEDS TO BE INCLUDED IN A NEW SYSTEM.

- DEVELOPED AN ACTION PLAN ABOUT 'HOW TO DO IT'.

- DEVELOPED AN ACTION PLAN TO IDENTIFY SUBORDINATES' TRAINING NEEDS.

1

PERFORMANCE APPRAISAL – INTRODUCTION

note	Welcome particpants to the course. Quickly ensure that everyone know the facilities. Cover:
	<ul><li>Toilets</li><li>Telephone</li><li>Messages</li><li>Emergency exits</li><li>Food and drink arrangements</li><li>'Special needs'.</li></ul>
	If participants have special needs – especially for meals, ensure that these are taken care of during the first coffee break.
text	I'D NOW LIKE YOU TO TAKE A LOOK AT THE COURSE SCHEDULE I SENT YOU. THINK ABOUT IT, AND THE REASONS FOR THIS COURSE.
	I'D LIKE YOU TO WRITE DOWN YOUR EXPECTATIONS OF THIS COURSE. WRITE DOWN THE TWO MOST IMPORTANT OUTCOMES YOU PERSONALLY WANT FROM THE NEXT TWO DAYS.
note	Allow a couple of minutes. Ask each person for their 'wants'. Make a note of them, to be referred to during the course, and in the end-of-course review.
text	I KNOW YOU'VE ALL SEEN THE COURSE OBJECTIVES IN THE MATERIAL I SENT OUT TO YOU WITH YOUR PRE-WORK. I'D LIKE TO TAKE ANOTHER LOOK TO CHECK THESE AGAINST YOUR OWN EXPECTATIONS.
V	Course objectives
note	Talk through objectives, explaining how each element contributes.
	Keep in mind previous responses about expectations. Where these are clearly at odds with objectives and what will happen in the course, discuss with the relevant participant/s.
	Work through the course schedule, indicating what happens when (and how), and how each element contributes to the objectives.
	Clear any questions.

fp text 2

PEOPLE HAVE A RIGHT TO THREE THINGS AT WORK

- TELL ME WHAT TO DO
- GIVE ME THE TOOLS TO DO IT
- TELL ME HOW I AM DOING.

WHY WE DO

- CAN BE TIED TO PROMOTION
- CAN HELP WITH PAY (RISES)
- TO 'MEASURE' HOW WELL SOMEONE IS WORKING
- TO GIVE 'DISCIPLINED' FEEDBACK TO PEOPLE ABOUT PERFORMANCE
- TO HELP IDENTIFY WHERE PEOPLE ARE HAVING DIFFICULTY AT WORK
- TO MAKE SURE MANAGERS AND SUBORDINATES *TALK* ABOUT 'PERFORMANCE'
- TO GIVE CONSISTENCY IN *MANAGING* PERFORMANCE
- CAN BE USED IN CAREER PLANNING
- CAN BE USED/TIED TO TRAINING NEEDS ANALYSIS
- CAN IDENTIFY AND ISOLATE AREAS OF GOOD AND BAD PERFORMANCE.

WHEN WE DON'T

- MORE ARGUMENTS ABOUT 'WHO IS BETTER' FOR PROMOTION
- CONFRONTING POOR PERFORMANCE IS EASIER TO AVOID
- APPRAISING PERFORMANCE CAN BECOME A SECRET PROCESS
- DISCUSSING PERFORMANCE CAN BECOME TABOO
- PERFORMANCE CAN GO UNMANAGED
- PEOPLE ARE LEFT IN DOUBT ABOUT HOW WELL THEY ARE WORKING
- PEOPLE ARE IN MORE DOUBT ABOUT HOW THEY CAN DEVELOP THEIR CAREERS
- MANAGERS AND SUBORDINATES DO NOT TALK ABOUT IMPORTANT THINGS LIKE TRAINING NEEDS, CAREER ASPIRATIONS
- WHETHER PEOPLE 'GET ON' IN AN ORGANIZATION CAN BE MORE A MATTER OF PERSONALITY RATHER THAN PERFORMANCE
- PEOPLE BECOME CONFUSED ABOUT CRITERIA FOR PROMOTION, TRAINING, ETC.

Writing the detail

2

WHY USE AN APPRAISAL SYSTEM?

text	WHAT I'D LIKE US TO DO FIRST IS ASCERTAIN SOME OF THE REASONS WHY AN ORGANIZATION ACTUALLY WANTS AN APPRAISAL SYSTEM. LET'S FACE IT. THEY ARE *ALWAYS* A HASSLE IN SOME WAY OR ANOTHER. FOR MANY PEOPLE THEY SEEM TO BE ABOUT AS POPULAR AS A BAD SMELL IN A LIFT!
	WHAT I'D LIKE US TO DO IS 'BRAINSTORM' SOME IDEAS ABOUT WHY AN ORGANIZATION – WHY WE WANT OR NEED A PERFORMANCE APPRAISAL SYSTEM.
	NOW JUST TO MAKE SURE WE UNDERSTAND BRAINSTORM – IT'S ONLY A MATTER OF THINKING OF AS MANY IDEAS ABOUT THE SUBJECT AS WE CAN. WE PUT THEM UP ON THE BOARD. WE *DO NOT* SAY WHETHER THEY'RE ANY GOOD OR NOT UNTIL WE'VE FINISHED.
	OK – WHY DO WE NEED ONE? WHAT CAN WE DO, OR DO BETTER IF WE HAVE AN APPRAISAL SYSTEM? WHAT HAPPENS IF WE DON'T HAVE ONE.
	OH – BY THE WAY – LET'S NOT TALK ABOUT WHAT HAPPENS WITH POOR SYSTEMS – THOSE THAT GIVE US TROUBLE. LET'S JUST CONCENTRATE ON THE WHYS OF USING A GOOD SYSTEM.
note	Use two flipcharts to record the group's answers. One should be labelled 'Why we use one', the other – 'What happens when we don't'.
	If participants are slow in starting up, offer an example or two. Ensure that the examples on the facing page are covered.
text	WELL, WE CAN SEE THAT THERE ARE SOME POWERFUL REASONS FOR USING A PERFORMANCE APPRAISAL SYSTEM. THERE ARE SOME POWERFUL REASONS FOR GETTING IT RIGHT. NOW LET'S SEE WHICH OF THESE YOU FEEL ARE MORE IMPORTANT THAN OTHERS. WHICH SHOULD WE CONCENTRATE ON FIRST WHEN DESIGNING A SYSTEM?
	WHAT WE'LL DO IS NUMBER THESE 1, 2, OR 3 WHERE 1 IS MOST IMPORTANT, 3 – LEAST. WHAT DO YOU THINK?
note	Gather in responses from the group. Write in appropriate numbers alongside the brainstormed list as participants discuss and agree. As participants suggest 1, 2, or 3, ask 'why?'
text	NOW BEFORE WE DISCUSS HOW OUR SYSTEM MEASURES UP TO THESE POINTS WE'VE RAISED, I'D LIKE US TO DO A LITTLE MORE WORK – THIS TIME IN SMALLER GROUPS.

fp text 3

SYNDICATE BRIEF

Appraisal is an emotional event. The results can significantly affect your relationship with your boss, your progress, motivation and your work.

How you *feel* just before, during, and after your appraisal is conducted is clearly important to the way you approach your work, and of course, to your performance.

Syndicate 1
Think back to your experiences. How did you actually *feel* about the whole thing? Why? What was the effect of feeling that way (before, during and after the appraisal process)?

Discuss this in your syndicates. Use the words that best describe your 'emotional response'.

List the key points on flipcharts, both positive and negative.

Be prepared to explain when and how these feelings occur, as well as the consequences.

Be frank; with yourself and your syndicate team. The results of your discussions are important to the success of any future system.

Syndicate 2
Think about your subordinate managers, when they are being appraised by you. Put yourself in their shoes for a moment.

How do you think they *felt* about the whole thing? Why? What do you think was the effect of those feelings (before, during and after the event)?

Discuss your views in your syndicate. Use words that best describe their 'emotional response'.

List these on flipcharts – both positive and negative.

Be prepared to explain when and how these feelings might have arisen, as well as your perception of the consequences.

Be frank – with yourself and your syndicate team. The results will be important to the success of any future system.

25–30 mins + 40.

3

HOW DO PEOPLE FEEL ABOUT APPRAISAL?

text	WHAT WE'LL DO NOW IS BREAK INTO TWO GROUPS TO ANSWER A QUESTION. NOW – THE QUESTION EACH GROUP IS ASKED TO ANSWER IS MORE OR LESS THE SAME – BUT NOT QUITE, SO I'D LIKE YOU NOT TO DISCUSS IT WITH YOUR 'OPPOSING' GROUP. YOU'LL SEE WHY LATER.
note	Break the group into two syndicates. Tell them where they will be working. Issue the syndicate brief/s. Make sure the syndicates see only one of the briefs.
HO	Syndicate task – 'How do they *feel* about *their* performance being appraised?'
text	BY THE WAY – IN ALL SYNDICATE TASKS I'D LIKE YOU FIRST TO SELECT SOMEONE TO 'CHAIR' YOUR WORK, AND SOMEONE ELSE TO ACT AS SCRIBE – TO WRITE ON YOUR FLIPCHARTS WHAT YOU HAVE AGREED. YOUR CHAIRPERSON WILL BE THE ONE WHO REPORTS BACK ON BEHALF OF THE SYNDICATE. I'D LIKE YOU TO ROTATE THE ROLES WITH EACH EXERCISE. OK, CAN YOU GO TO YOUR SYNDICATE AREAS, AND ANSWER THE QUESTION. I'LL BE AROUND IN A WHILE TO HELP YOU, IF YOU NEED IT. WE'LL GET BACK TOGETHER AGAIN IN ABOUT 25 MINUTES.
note	Check with syndicates to ensure they understand what they need to do. Try to help them use appropriate language (emotion words) to explain 'feelings'. Try to make sure that negative feelings are identified, whether reasonable/unreasonable, dealt with or not, whether they came later or at the time. Do not restrict the exercise to negative feelings only. It is important to explore the impact and meaning of both. Reconvene after 25 minutes. Compare and discuss responses. Discuss the perceived situation giving rise to the feelings described. If the results from the two syndicates are different, explore why that perception should exist. Likewise, if the results are similar. Are the two groups (senior managers and their subordinates) perceived to feel the same/different? Why? Are perceptions realistic? Do not discuss what could be done, or done better. That will be dealt with later. Conclude by agreeing and recording a 'consensus view' about 'feelings'. Post flipcharts on wall.

Writing the detail

4

THE CURRENT SYSTEM

text	NOW WE'RE GOING TO LOOK AT SOME OF THE WORK YOU DID BEFORE THE COURSE. WE'RE GOING TO DEAL WITH YOUR DISCUSSIONS WITH YOUR OWN MANAGERS ABOUT THE CURRENT PERFORMANCE APPRAISAL SYSTEM.
	THE WAY WE'RE GOING TO DO THIS IS ONCE AGAIN TO BREAK INTO SYNDICATES – THIS TIME THREE.
HO	Syndicate task – strengths and weaknesses of the current system.
note	Talk through the syndicate brief.
text	IN YOUR SYNDICATES I'D LIKE YOU TO DISCUSS WHAT HAPPENED. WHAT DID THEY SAY? WHAT DID YOU THINK? WERE VIEWS DIFFERENT? SURPRISING? FINALLY I'D LIKE YOU TO AGREE A LIST OF THE STRENGTHS AND WEAKNESSES OF THE SYSTEM. WE'LL GET BACK TOGETHER AGAIN IN ABOUT THIRTY MINUTES TO CHECK ON THE RESULTS.
note	Break the group into three syndicates. Keep in touch with syndicates to ensure understanding of the task and openness of discussions and outputs. Persist in exploring statements of strengths and weaknesses by asking 'Why' they feel that way. Ask the group to try to cite examples of actual events in appraisal which have given rise to their views. Agree a final list of strengths and weaknesses.
	Attach finished flipcharts to wall, alongside those produced after the previous exercise.
text	OK, WE'VE DISCUSSED WHY ORGANIZATIONS, INCLUDING US, USE PERFORMANCE APPRAISAL, AND WE'VE DISCUSSED HOW PEOPLE ACTUALLY FEEL ABOUT IT IN OUR COMPANY. WE'VE NOW LOOKED AT WHAT SEEMS TO BE GOOD AND NOT SO GOOD ABOUT THE APPRAISAL SYSTEM WE USE RIGHT NOW.
	LOOK AT THE LAST TWO SETS OF FLIPCHARTS. WHAT ARE THE PROBLEMS WE SEEM TO NEED TO RESOLVE?
note	Discuss and agree problems. Record agreements on flipcharts, post alongside other flipcharts.

In reading through what I have written, I am even more uneasy about how little it has taken to write a morning's session. Have I put in enough text? Should I include more inputs from the front before banging away at the syndicate exercises? I will have to think about that a little.

I could do with more space and spaces. My squint test does not quite work. Maybe I could rewrite text 3 as two pages, the second as the syndicate debrief, with more text, and some ideas for the debrief on the facing page.

I can put some of my ideas of 'problems', gleaned from observing syndicate work, on the facing page of what is now text page 4. I can use these notes in finalizing discussions at this point, *and* in directing discussions in the next session.

No doubt after all this instruction, to which you have surely paid careful attention, you could think of heaps of other improvements. If you can, try them out. See how the alternatives you come up with alter the images and information that the pages give you.

In my final rewrite (Appendix C) I have written nine pages of text instead of these four. I feel more comfortable about how I've covered time and content. The timetable for these pages is also in the appendix. So are my *final* comments about this last example. But before you check the rewrite, write your own version. See how they compare.

Let us move on. There is not a great deal more to be said about the last two parts of the manual – so I will be brief for a change.

7 Finally

SUPPORT DOCUMENTATION

This is the last but one (or penultimate, if you like long words) part of the manual (see Figure 2.3). It contains copies of all the paper associated with the course.

Once again, it is about being tidy and disciplined, and 'writing for someone else'. When you are preparing for the course, and leafing through the course outline and detailed text, you will not want to be searching archives or the dim, dark and dusty recesses of a storeroom to find out what a particular handout, syndicate exercise, or case study is about. The information should be at your fingertips.

If you have run the course before, you will be thinking about the experience, working through your timetable, remembering what did not go as you intended. Leafing through the material in your support papers will be an important part of effective decision making for 'next time'. You will be more inclined to do that if it is all in one place, and readily available. (Sometimes we find pressing reasons for not disturbing ourselves from our chairs to look something up. The promise to yourself to do it later is oft broken.) Even if you do have a central 'store' where case studies and so on are kept, I urge you to keep copies in your training manual. How often do we go to the central store only to find that the cupboard is bare? One of our colleagues has forgotten to inform people that the last copy (of the most difficult or hard to remember item) has been used.

Keep your own supply, and you will never be disappointed.

ODDS 'N ENDS

This last part of the manual is a sort of general receptacle for material which does not really fit anywhere else. If you want to use only one section – support papers – then go ahead. However, you may learn to love the usefulness of a category that can accommodate the odds and ends.

When you cannot find that article on killer wales under 'K' or 'W', you will know it is in Odds 'n Ends. It is the last resort of the clever filing system that recognizes that everything does not fit into the neat little boxes we create for things.

8 Using the manual

I will not apologise for repeating much of what has been said before. After all, is not repetition one of the cornerstones of learning?

You will not know how powerful the format is until you have really used it. The following information about using the manual falls into three categories:

- Preparing for a course;
- Running the course;
- Reviewing the course.

Let us begin at the beginning.

PREPARATION

The first, and perhaps most obvious use of the manual is the help it gives you in course design. The disciplines of the process ensures that you really think things through; down to and including visualizing actual events, people's reactions, your reactions to their reactions, and so on.

When you have gone through the process I have been describing you will already be so well prepared that you will be frightening! When you get to running the course you will hardly need your manual at all. In your head, you have already run the course. And of course when you did you did it perfectly. You will be brimful of confidence.

Your manual will have its visuals and facing pages with your 'summaries of summaries' of key elements of the material. You will have your own brief, informal notes in these areas – as sketchy as you like. You will have your text as a fall-back reference, to look at in 'down time', those occasions when you are not directly juggling with the collective intellects of hoards of eager participants, each aching to be transformed.

You will have your timetable – the briefest of all summaries.

You will know, with certainty, where everything is: every note, handout, syndicate exercise, reference paper, visual, comma and full stop. (Well almost.)

As I have said – many times – you will hardly need the manual. But! It is there to be used. It is designed to be used. So use it.

The last activity you carry out, as you prepare for the course, is to read through the manual again. While you are doing this highlight the key words and phrases in your text, those you have wrapped in your own brilliant 'real talking language'. Only the key words, mind. You will lose impact if you highlight everything. Use yellow highlighter pen. Black on yellow is a good colour combination to see. In Appendix C, a rewrite of the performance appraisal example, the words and phrases I highlighted at this point are shown in bold.

While you are reading through the manual, assiduously highlighting, you might make some pencil notes on your copies of visuals, and on other 'facing pages'. Just be careful not to clutter the pages. Do not remove the impact of space and spaces you have built in so well. Why pencil? Because the notes you want on these pages refer only to the next course. You may want to change them from event to event. It is easier to do this with pencil than it is with ink, or chipped granite, is it not?

When you have done that – you are ready to roll!

RUNNING THE COURSE

On the day, place your manual on the table (the one you keep all your trainer junk on) at a slight angle. You can see it a little easier; from either a standing or sitting position. Do not make the angle too high, as on a lectern. I think it is inappropriate for the greater informality of a training room. It might form part of a shield between you and the trainees, and you do not want that do you?

Take out the relevant timetable and place it alongside the manual. Put a pencil alongside that. You will need that to make notes of the actual times the material takes to run through. You will need these notes for the next time you prepare. I generally have my actual visuals – overhead transparencies – in the manual, at the relevant page. As long as you know where they are . . . .

Do not worry about note dependency. You are setting up safeguards, not crutches. You will have oodles of confidence. That will make you mobile, dynamic. You will be able to 'join the group' as often as you like. You will be great.

On occasions when you need to refer to your detailed notes and there is no 'down time' you will be able to see your key words from nine miles away. (That is a bit of a fib, but you *will* be able to see it from several feet, or a metre or so in new money, *if* your eyesight is similar to mine.)

If people do spot the occasional closer reference to your material they will not frown upon it. They will not think you do not know what you are doing. They will respect your professionalism in making sure you give them the best, and that you have really prepared.

I had some feedback once, through a colleague, about a course I ran for a particularly hardnosed bunch of line managers. (Feedback that told me something about 'the manual', that is.) The feedback was from them, about my performance. In essence, it was 'He had lots of notes, but never referred to them.' (For the participants that meant I knew my subject. For me it reinforced the value of my preparation.) Well, I did refer to them – often. It just did not show. The positive feedback made me feel warm and fuzzy.

When times or events differ from planned, or your material does not seem to work, make your pencilled notes in the appropriate place. Nothing elaborate. Just enough to remind you about what happened when you next review the course.

REVIEW

When you have run the course, leaf through the manual. Remind yourself of actual timing and events. You will *know* how things went compared with plan. Your complete plan is there, together with your incisive notes on the living, breathing pages of your manual. You will know what to look out for next time.

This does not mean you have to change anything. It means you can consider what might need changing. If you do need to modify anything, you will not need to plough through everything – only those specific parts you have been able to identify clearly. Whether you modify or not will depend on the total dynamics of the past event; the idiosyncrasies of the participants, the environment, and your actual performance.

Next time you run through your preparation, your manual, pencilled comments, timetable – all will make the last course as fresh as yesterday in your memory. Your preparation for the next course will be even more certain.

So will a good performance.

Appendix A: Presentation techniques example

There are three pages of text in the rewrite that follows. We might have managed with two, if we had preferred it). The copy of the visual (V1) in the original example has had some handwritten notes added by the trainer just to prick my memory a little more. (It is now V3.)

The rewrite has more words, and more spaces. The squint test talks more strongly. It did not take much longer to write really. It left much less to chance or memory.

There is not much 'stage direction' in the notes. The text takes care of that.

The three pages would take about 20 minutes to work through: text 1 – 1 minute, text 2 – about 12–15 minutes, and text 3, about 5–7 minutes.

See what you think.

V1

Presentations

Appendix A: Presentation techniques example

1

PRESENTATION TECHNIQUES – INTRODUCTION

note	The objective of the presentations session is that participants will be able to make their presentations according to the same model/guidelines. They will contribute to how this model is formed.
text	FOR THE NEXT HOUR OR SO WE'LL BE TALKING ABOUT PRESENTATIONS. WE'LL ALSO SEE A FILM ABOUT IT.
	FOR THE PURPOSES OF THIS SESSION 'PRESENTATION' SIMPLY MEANS STANDING UP AND TALKING FORMALLY TO A GROUP OF PEOPLE.
	SOMETHING LIKE THIS.
V1	Presentations
text	MOST OF YOU ALREADY DO THIS FROM TIME TO TIME – TALKING TO CUSTOMERS OR STAFF, ROTARIANS OR VOTERS ....
	WELL DURING THIS COURSE YOU'LL ALL BE MAKING PRESENTATIONS – TO THE GROUP, TO US 'UP FRONT', AND TO THE GUESTS WE'LL HAVE DOWN HERE.
	WHEN YOU TELL US ABOUT YOUR BOOK REVIEW; EVERY TIME YOU GIVE US SOME FEEDBACK FROM YOUR SMALL GROUP WORK; WE'LL WANT YOU TO PUT SOME POLISH AND ZIP INTO IT.
	YOU'LL BE MAKING 'PRESENTATIONS' HERE.
	WITH THIS IN MIND WE'LL DEVELOP SOME GUIDELINES FOR YOU TO FOLLOW WHEN PREPARING AND MAKING YOUR PRESENTATIONS.
	THEY'LL ALSO HELP AFTER THE COURSE WHEN YOU MAKE PRESENTATIONS IN THE FUTURE.

fp 2

IMPORTANT FACTORS

Preparation

PURPOSE AND OBJECTIVES
KNOW THE MATERIAL
HOW MUCH MATERIAL TO INCLUDE?
WHAT SHAPE/STRUCTURE IS BEST?
VISUALS, PICTURES, DIAGRAMS, CHARTS, GRAPHS
WHAT PROCESS?
WHAT KIND OF ROOM?
SURROUNDINGS
NOISE
INTERRUPTIONS
SETTING
FITTINGS
HISTORY – DOES THIS FIT?
TIMING – IS THIS THE RIGHT TIME?
AUDIENCE – KNOWLEDGE NOW, EXPECTATIONS, NEEDS, FRIENDLY/HOSTILE, NUMBERS . . .?
NOTES AND STRUCTURE
REHEARSAL

Presentation

PACE AND TIMING
NOTES/NOTES FORMAT
CLOCK
WATER
EYE CONTACT
VOICE CONTROL
INTERRUPTIONS
QUESTIONS
FEEDBACK

Review

HOW DID IT GO?
WHAT TO CHANGE – WHY?
WHAT TO KEEP IN – WHY?

PRESENTATIONS – IMPORTANT FACTORS

text	NOW THERE ARE A NUMBER OF IMPORTANT FACTORS TO BEAR IN MIND WHEN MAKING A PRESENTATION. QUITE A FEW THINGS YOU NEED TO THINK ABOUT IF YOU WANT TO GET YOUR MESSAGE ACROSS.
	SO BEGIN WITH I'D LIKE YOU ALL TO THINK ABOUT IT FOR A FEW MINUTES. I'D LIKE YOU TO MAKE A LIST OF THE THINGS YOU THINK ARE 'IMPORTANT'. THINGS TO THINK ABOUT BEFORE THE PRESENTATION, DURING IT, AND EVEN AFTERWARDS.
	FOR INSTANCE – REALLY KNOWING YOUR MATERIAL, THE TIME IT WILL TAKE, THE PEOPLE YOU'LL BE TALKING TO, WHETHER YOU'LL BE USING VISUAL AIDS, HOW YOU'LL KNOW HOW WELL YOU'RE DOING, AND SO ON.
	WHAT DO YOU THINK THEY MIGHT BE? WRITE DOWN YOUR IDEAS IN ANY ORDER, AND IN A FEW MINUTES WE'LL SEE WHAT THEY ARE, AND HOW THEY COMPARE.
note	Give participants about five minutes to jot down some ideas.
text	OK – LET'S TAKE A LOOK AT WHAT YOU THINK. AS YOU TELL ME WHAT YOU'VE WRITTEN I'M GOING TO SEPARATE THEM INTO THREE GROUPS;
	THE THINGS YOU DO BEFORE THE PRESENTATION;
	WHAT YOU NEED TO PAY ATTENTION TO DURING IT;
	AND/AFTER THE PRESENTATION.
note	Ask participants to give you their ideas. Clarify their meaning where needed. Write the ideas on flips according to the 'before, during, and after' structure.
	Discuss the factors briefly as they are listed. Ensure that the completed flips include the ideas listed on the facing page.

V3

PREPARE AND PLAN

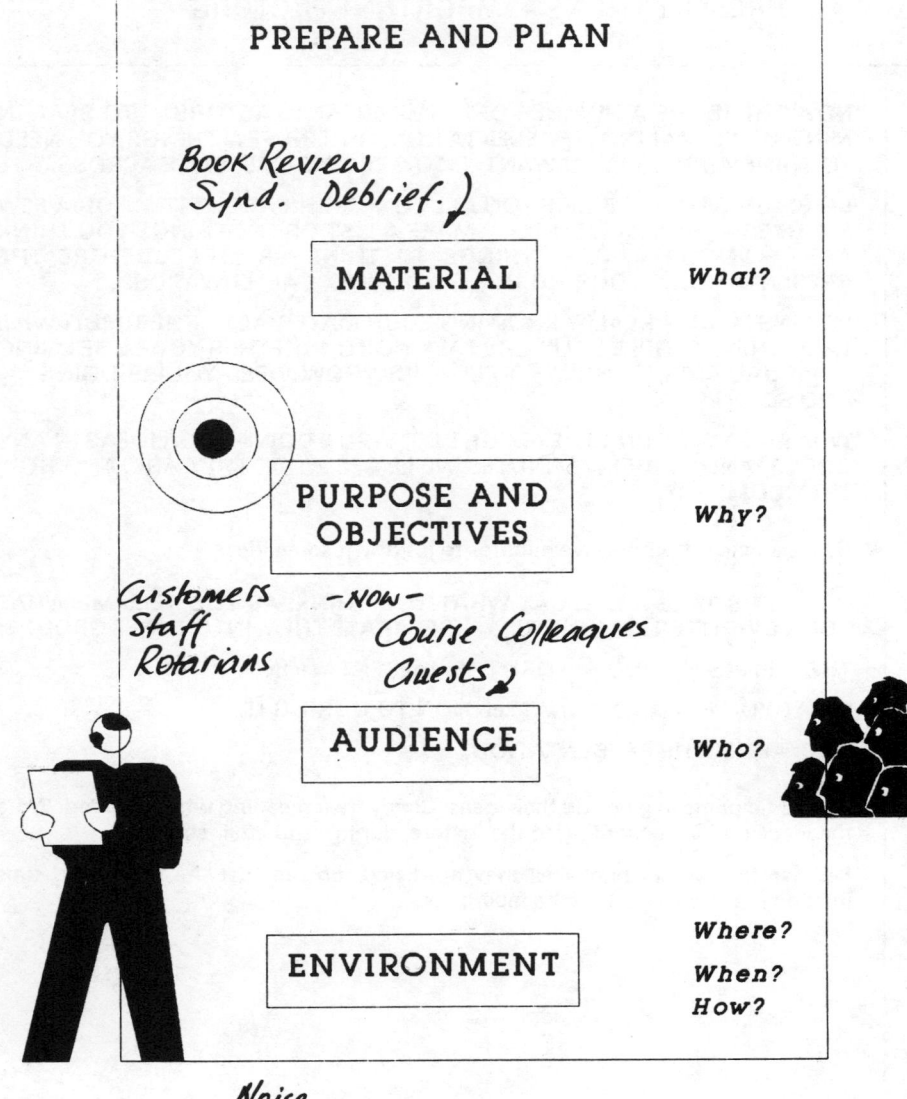

Book Review
Synd. Debrief.)

| **MATERIAL** | What? |

| **PURPOSE AND OBJECTIVES** | Why? |

Customers　*—NOW—*
Staff　*Course Colleagues*
Rotarians　*Guests*

| **AUDIENCE** | Who? |

| **ENVIRONMENT** | Where? When? How? |

Noise
Heat
Privacy
People
Light
Time

Appendix A: Presentation techniques example

3

PREPARATION – ESPECIALLY YOURSELF

text	WE CAN SEE BY THE LISTS WE'VE COMPILED THAT MOST OF 'THE IMPORTANT FACTORS' WE'VE BEEN TALKING ABOUT RELATE TO THINGS WE NEED TO THINK ABOUT BEFORE THE PRESENTATION. IN FACT, THE KEY TO SUCCESSFUL PRESENTATIONS IS THE PREPARATION – THE PLANNING YOU DO BEFORE THE EVENT. THE BETTER THIS IS, THE BETTER YOUR PRESENTATION.
V3	Prepare and plan
HO	Prepare and plan
note	Issue a copy of the visual to participants.
text	HERE'S A COPY OF THE VISUAL I'M SHOWING. IT SHOWS SOME OF THE MAIN POINTS TO THINK ABOUT IN YOUR PREPARATION. WHAT I'D LIKE YOU TO DO NOW IS MAKE A NOTE OF THE ITEMS ON OUR FLIPCHARTS THAT FIT AGAINST THE HEADINGS ON YOUR COPY. WHEN YOU'VE FINISHED THAT YOU'LL HAVE A ROUGH CHECKLIST TO HELP WITH YOUR LATER PRESENTATIONS.
note	Help participants where needed. Make the kind of notes you are suggesting on the visual being shown (using water-base pens). The activity should not take more than five minutes.
text	BEFORE WE MOVE ON TO TALK A LITTLE MORE ABOUT PREPARATION I'D LIKE TO STRESS THE IMPORTANCE OF PREPARING YOURSELF. YOUR OWN ATTITUDE, IF YOU DON'T WORK AT IT, CAN BE A PROBLEM. HOW YOU FEEL ABOUT MAKING A PRESENTATION WILL SHOW UP ON THE DAY. I'M TALKING ABOUT 'NERVES'. EVEN THE BEST PRESENTERS GET NERVOUS. OR SHOULD I SAY ESPECIALLY THE BEST PRESENTERS? PEOPLE LIKE ROBERT MENZIES AND WINSTON CHURCHILL WERE SAID TO BECOME QUITE ILL WITH NERVES BEFORE MAKING A 'BIG ONE'. NOW I DON'T PROPOSE THAT IT'S NATURAL TO BECOME ILL BUT I DO SAY THAT AN ATTACK OF THE WOBBLIES IS NATURAL. I KNOW I GET THEM, AND I NEED SOME HELP TO OVERCOME THEM. BEING NERVOUS IS NORMAL AND NATURAL SO DON'T WORRY. A LACK OF 'NERVES' MAY BE A SIGN THAT YOU DON'T CARE ENOUGH ABOUT YOUR AUDIENCE OR YOUR MATERIAL. PEOPLE WHO DON'T CARE ENOUGH DON'T DO WELL ENOUGH. LET'S MOVE ON.

How does that seem? Remember, this is only a mini-teach. Nothing will be covered in much depth, so do not worry about the actual content.

Let us work quickly through the three pages of text.

The first general point I would like to make is that I have increased the use of space; both between blocks of text, and within the sentences themselves. This tends to highlight the key words and phrases. (This is further enhanced by the use of a highligher pen on a finished manual.)

How much space you put into your text depends on how much room you actually have, and your own personal preferences. It depends on what works for you.

Another general point needs to be made. Each page of text should have a logical end point. The format does not work if your text merely runs on without regard to this. At the very least your last words on the page should give you a natural 'breathing space'; a break where you can glance down at the page quite naturally, if you need to.

In this example I have used the separation of ideas as the break. Where one idea or theme needs longer treatment, then you must look for a natural break in the structure of that theme. This must be kept in mind when planning your pages of text.

Where your idea or theme runs over more than one page of text – as it often will – the way you title the pages will help you to keep in touch with how much you are going to be delivering. Earlier I used an example timetable to illustrate this ('Motivation – Maslow – 1, Motivation – Maslow – 2').

Now for further comments on the contents of the three pages.

In text page 1 I have put in a modest objective for the session. This will help to keep me on track, both as I write the material, and as I deliver it. The participants' presentations during the rest of the course will determine whether or not this objective is achieved.

The text attempts to tie in the subject with what participants already know or have experienced. It also sets up the reason for including this session. I do not want to have to spend a lot of time legitimizing it. If I have only one hour to deal with the subject, I had better encourage them to listen right away.

In text page 2 there is a 'more work and less words' ratio. There is less formal input from the trainer.

The timeplan will indicate how long you might be spending, 'clarifying ideas' and 'discussing the factors'. If you are fifteen minutes away from your planned end of this page when you get to this part, then you have that long to work on it. If the group needs more, or less, time your timeplan will be telling you to hurry up or slow down, or that you are going to have to modify some of your later material.

In text page 3 it may take more time for participants to write down their lists on the copy of the visual they have. It depends on how much is generated (and of course how fast they can write!). You will have your timeplan to hand so you will know how much time you can give to the exercise, and the impact of over- or underrun.

Finally, I would like to discuss again how much text your write and its relationship with how much – or what you might say. Take, for example, one paragraph from text page 3.

Appendix A: Presentation techniques example

NOW I DON'T PROPOSE THAT IT'S NATURAL TO BECOME ILL BUT I DO SAY THAT AN ATTACK OF THE WOBBLIES IS NATURAL. I KNOW I GET THEM, AND I NEED SOME HELP TO OVERCOME THEM. BEING NERVOUS IS NORMAL AND NATURAL SO DON'T WORRY.

On the day I might actually say . . .

NOW I'M NOT SUGGESTING THAT IT'S NATURAL FOR *EVERYBODY* TO THROW UP, OR WHATEVER. BUT IT IS NATURAL FOR PEOPLE TO GET AN ATTACK OF THE WOBBLIES TO SOME EXTENT OR ANOTHER.

I GUESS I MAKE QUITE A FEW 'PRESENTATIONS'. THIS IS ONE, ISN'T IT? NO MATTER HOW OFTEN I DO IT, I'M ALWAYS CONCERNED ABOUT WHAT WILL HAPPEN. I STILL GET AN ATTACK OF NERVES SOMETIMES. HOW MUCH OR HOW BADLY DEPENDS ON WHAT I'M GOING TO TALK ABOUT – HOW CONFIDENT I AM THAT I HAVE EVERYTHING UNDER CONTROL – AND WHO I'M GOING TO BE TALKING TO. THE OLD ADRENALINE STARTS PUMPING THROUGH AND GETS YOU A BIT HYPED UP. IT HAPPENS TO EVERYONE – SO DON'T WORRY IF IT GETS TO YOU TOO.

It is likely that I will actually ask the group about whether anyone *does* experience nervousness before making a presentation; ask them how they feel, and why they think they might feel that way. I might ask what the consequences have been.

Precisely what I will say on the day will depend . . . on the group and their reactions or apparent needs. It will depend on the time – do I need to stretch or shrink the session at this point? I have a number of options, but I have my key words written in a way that I understand at a glance, in a format that will tell me the impact of taking a specific option.

See what I mean?

Appendix B: Quality customer service example

There are two pages of text and two visuals in this rewrite.

The purpose and timing of this session is spelled out for the line manager-deliverer.

There is plenty of space.

Text page 21 may take more than the five minutes allotted. It is really only to encourage syndicates to move in the right direction. The trainer will be working in the syndicates helping them to develop their responses in the desired method.

V21

Issue

Staff experience	STAFF ARE TOO JUNIOR. THEY DON'T KNOW ENOUGH ABOUT OUR WORK. THEY NEED MORE EXPERIENCE.
	AND/OR
	THE PEOPLE I'VE GOT HAVE ONLY HAD HEAD OFFICE EXPERIENCE. THEY DON'T KNOW HOW TO WORK IN THE FRONT LINE.
Staff levels	WE DON'T HAVE ENOUGH JUNIOR STAFF. WE HAVE MORE SUPERVISORS THAN WE NEED, BUT THEY WON'T DO JUNIOR WORK.
	AND/OR
	THERE'S TOO MUCH WORK TO DO. WE'RE OK FOR MOST OF THE DAY, BUT AT PEAK HOURS . . .
Staff quality	WE'RE NOT EMPLOYING ENOUGH QUALITY STAFF. WE SHOULD CHANGE OUR RECRUITING POLICY OR . . .
	WE NEED MORE TRAINING, AND MORE RELEVANT TRAINING (FOR INSTANCE . . .).
Conditions	THE LAYOUT OF OUR WORK AREA DOESN'T ALLOW US TO IMPROVE SERVICE. IT NEEDS AN OVERHAUL.
Equipment	OUR COMPUTER EQUIPMENT IS TOO SLOW. IT TAKES TOO LONG TO ACCESS INFORMATION CUSTOMERS NEED. IT CREATES EXTRA WORK.

Appendix B: Quality customer service example

1

YES BUTS – INTRODUCTION

note	The purpose of this session is to identify and discuss barriers that will arise in implementing QCS in various areas of the company.
	Overview: Introduction 5 mins Syndicate work 30 mins Visual Debrief/Discussion 30 mins
text	DURING THE DAY SO FAR WE'VE BEEN MAKING A NOTE OF SOME OF YOUR CONCERNS ABOUT THE THINGS THAT YOU THINK WILL GET IN THE WAY OF IMPLEMENTING QUALITY CUSTOMER SERVICE IN YOUR AREA. THEY'RE THERE ON THE FLIPCHARTS AT THE BACK OF THE ROOM.
	WELL, NOW WE'RE GOING TO DEAL WITH THESE BLOCKS OR DIFFICULTIES AND ANY MORE YOU CAN THINK OF.
	WHEN WE'VE DONE THAT WE'LL LOOK AT SOME WAYS YOU CAN THINK OF TO OVERCOME THESE BLOCKS OR DIFFICULTIES.
	WE'RE NOW GOING TO DO SOME WORK IN SYNDICATES. I WANT YOU TO THINK ABOUT WHAT THE PROBLEMS ARE. I DON'T WANT TO DEAL WITH ANY POTENTIAL SOLUTIONS AT THIS STAGE – JUST MAKE SURE THAT WE CAN AGREE WHAT IT IS THAT WE THINK WILL GET IN THE WAY.
	I WANT YOU TO 'LABEL AND DESCRIBE' THE PROBLEM ISSUES. THAT MEANS PUTTING SOME SORT OF TITLE OR 'LABEL' TO AN ISSUE, AND, TO MAKE SURE THAT WE ARE TALKING ABOUT THE SAME – OR DIFFERENT THINGS, DESCRIBING WHAT CONCERNS YOU IN A LITTLE MORE DETAIL.
	LIKE THIS, FOR EXAMPLE.
V21	Example of 'Label and describe'.
note	Work briefly through the visual ensuring the group understands how to 'label and describe' the issues. The trainer will assist if needed.

V22

In your syndicates:

- APPOINT A SPOKESPERSON TO REPORT BACK TO THE WHOLE GROUP.

- APPOINT A SCRIBE TO MAKE NOTES ON YOUR FLIPCHARTS OF WHAT YOU AGREE NEEDS TO BE ADDRESSED.

- USING THE FORMAT DESCRIBED – ANSWER THE QUESTION

  'WHAT IS GOING TO MAKE IT DIFFICULT FOR US TO IMPLEMENT QUALITY CUSTOMER SERVICE PRINCIPLES AND ACTIONS IN OUR/MY AREA?'

You have 30 minutes to complete your work.

DO NOT TALK SOLUTIONS. WE'LL DEAL WITH THESE WHEN WE'VE FULLY DESCRIBED THE ISSUES OF CONCERN.

WHEN YOU'VE COMPLETED THE EXERCISE FIX YOUR FLIPCHARTS TO THE WALLS OF THE TRAINING ROOM.

QUICKLY REVIEW THE WORK OF THE OTHER SYNDICATES.

Appendix B: Quality customer service example

22

YES BUTS – SYNDICATE EXERCISE

text	THIS KIND OF 'SO WHAT' EXERCISE. YOU MIGHT SAY THAT 'STAFF' IS A CONCERN YOU HAVE. SO WHAT? WHAT IS IT ABOUT STAFF THAT CAUSES CONCERN? WE'RE JUST LOOKING FOR A UNIFORM WAY TO IDENTIFY THE PROBLEMS SO THAT WE ALL UNDERSTAND THEM IN THE SAME WAY. IF WE CAN DO THAT, WE'RE MORE LIKELY TO BE ABLE TO DEAL WITH THEM TO EVERYONE'S SATISFACTION. OK. LET'S GET ON WITH THE SYNDICATE EXERCISE.
note	Break the group into three syndicates. Make sure that the group is balanced in terms of support, personality, positive/negative outlook, etc.
V22	Syndicate brief.
note	Talk through the visual, ensure that participants understand the brief. Tell them that you and the trainer will be moving around the syndicates to help where it's needed. (Ensure that when this happens you merely clarify the exercise. *Do not* offer your own ideas about either problems or solutions.) Ensure that participants do not discuss solutions. Reconvene after about 30 minutes. Give participants 10 minutes to review the work of other syndicates.
text	WHAT I'D LIKE US TO DO FIRST IS TO SEE WHERE YOU'VE IDENTIFIED THE SAME ISSUES AND, OF COURSE, DIFFERENT ISSUES. IN THIS WAY WE'LL BE ABLE TO SEE HOW WIDESPREAD OR SPECIFIC THESE ARE. WE'LL BE ABLE TO SEE WHERE PROBLEMS ARE OCCURRING MORE OFTEN. WHEN WE'VE DONE THAT WE'LL PUT THESE IN SOME SORT OF ORDER OF IMPORTANCE. THIS WILL HELP US IN OUR ACTION PLANNING, LATER. DON'T WORRY YET ABOUT SOLUTIONS. WE'LL SEE IN THE NEXT SESSION HOW OUR 'EFFECTIVE MANAGEMENT PRACTICES' WILL HELP OUT. FOR NOW – STICK WITH THE ISSUES.
note	Conduct a group discussion to clarify, or further describe the issues. Identify how many are common to many areas. When this has been done agree the relative importance of the issues.

Well – how did we do? I have checked back, and I think that I have attended to all the points listed for improvement. But what do you think?

There are a couple of comments I would like to make.

I would have liked a little more space in the second page. I think I could have created a better pattern for the squint test. On balance though, I thought it better to go with what I have rather than run on to another page. If I had decided to use another page I might have developed a model for 'setting priorities'. (Decisions lead to options; options to decisions.)

I have shuffled some information around and introduced the two visuals. They are a great comfort to me when I am running a course. It is amazing how quickly you can pick up information from them when you need it. They turn out to be great summaries (of the summaries in the text). Where I can justify a visual, I always use one in the manual. I do not have to use it in the course itself if it seems unnecessary or over the top.

The syndicate exercise will give the facilitators plenty of opportunity to confer on how to handle 'the next part'. With them floating around there will be ample opportunity to steer the exercise in the desired direction.

Well, that is enough of that. I am sure if I worked on it some more, I would find heaps of other ways to improve it.

Wouldn't I?

Appendix C: Performance appraisal example

Here are the nine pages of text and the timetable for the last rewrite. There are two visuals and three other facing pages. The timetable (at the very end of the appendix) shows that these pages will take us around three hours to work through.

Before you begin to read through this example, take the time to remind yourself of the background described. Reread the course summary. Compare this with your own notes and/or thoughts. Take your time. Work with the material.

Appendix C: Performance appraisal example

ADMINISTRATION AND INTRODUCTION

note

Welcome participants to the course. Ensure that everyone is familiar with the training centre's facilities and layout. Cover:

- Emergency exits and fire precautions
- Toilets
- Telephones
- Messages – message board
- Food and drink arrangements
- 'Special needs'.

If any participant has **'special needs'** (e.g. diet) ensure that these are noted and taken care of during the first coffee break.

text

BEFORE WE ACTUALLY GET UNDER WAY I THINK IT'S **IMPORTANT** TO MAKE SURE THAT WE CAN PUT THIS **COURSE INTO CONTEXT**.

SO WE CAN SEE EXACTLY HOW THIS FITS IN WITH ALL YOUR OTHER WORK.

AS YOU KNOW, THE **COMPANY** IS **CONSIDERING CHANGING** – IMPROVING THE PERFORMANCE **APPRAISAL SYSTEM** WE HAVE. WHAT'S MORE TO THE POINT, YOU **SENIOR MANAGERS** ARE GOING TO HAVE AN IMPORTANT **ROLE** IN THIS **PROCESS**.

YOU'RE GOING TO BE THE ONES WHO **SHAPE THE FINAL OUTCOME**.

THE **COURSE** IS PART OF THAT PROCESS. IT'S DESIGNED TO **HELP** YOU ALL **DECIDE HOW** YOU'RE GOING TO **WORK**, WHAT YOU'RE **GOING TO DO**, IN A WAY THAT YOU CAN ALL AGREE WITH, AND **WORK TOGETHER** ON – AS A **TEAM**.

I'M SURE THAT EACH ONE OF YOU IS LIKELY TO BE A BIT CONCERNED ABOUT SPENDING TWO DAYS AWAY FROM YOUR JOBS.

EVEN SO, BY THE TIME WE'VE FINISHED, YOU MAY FIND THAT **TWO DAYS IS HARDLY ENOUGH** – EVEN WITH THE WORK YOU'VE ALREADY DONE IN PREPARATION.

YOU'LL HAVE MADE THAT DECISION – AND SOME OTHERS – BY THE TIME WE FINISH TOMORROW AFTERNOON.

VISUAL TITLE (e.g. 'symbols')

| PRE-WORK | Orientation
Information gathering |

| WHY PERFORMANCE APPRAISAL | What's in it?
For whom? |

| OUR CURRENT SYSTEM | What do we have now? |

| IMPORTANT FACTORS | What seems to be important for success? |

| OTHER 'NEEDS' | |

| PRACTICE | The appraisal interview |

| ACTION PLANNING | Putting the course to work |

Appendix C: Performance appraisal example

2

COURSE STRUCTURE

text	YOU'VE ALL HAD A COPY OF THE COURSE SCHEDULE, AND I SUPPOSE YOU'VE HAD A CHANCE TO LOOK THROUGH IT. THE INFORMATION IS A BIT SKETCHY.
	I'D LIKE TO SHOW YOU SOME **MORE INFO**RMATION ABOUT IT TO GIVE YOU A BETTER IDEA OF WHAT WILL BE HAPPENING.
V2	**Course Structure**
note	Work through the diagram, covering:
text	WHAT WE HAVE HERE IS A **STEP-BY-STEP PROCESS** WHICH WILL HELP TO SORT THINGS OUT IN THE SHORTEST POSSIBLE TIME. IT'S DESIGNED TO MAKE SURE THAT WE **COVER** ALL OF THE **IMPORTANT POINTS** IN A WAY THAT BUILDS UP OUR UNDERSTANDING AND **AGREEMENT** ABOUT **THE WAY THINGS ARE**, AND WHAT **NEEDS TO BE DONE**.
	YOU'VE ALREADY TAKEN THE **FIRST STEP** IN YOUR **PRE-WORK**. THIS WAS SO YOU COULD BEGIN TO FORM SOME FIRMER OPINIONS ABOUT APPRAISAL, DISCOVER WHETHER THESE WERE MORE OR LESS IN LINE WITH THOSE OF YOUR TEAM, AND OF COURSE TO GIVE YOU ONE OR TWO NEW INSIGHTS.
	WE'LL BE **STARTING** THE DAY BY **EXPLORING** **WHY WE BOTHER**. WE'LL BE LOOKING AT WHAT'S IN IT FOR THE COMPANY, AND THE INDIVIDUALS WHO WORK IN IT. WHAT ARE WE TRYING TO GAIN? WE'LL BRIEFLY **EXPLORE** THE **IMPACT** OF WHAT WE'RE DOING NOW.
	OUR **NEXT** STEP WILL BE TO **LOOK AT** WHAT WE'VE GOT **NOW**. WE'LL SEE HOW THIS STACKS UP AGAINST WHAT WE MIGHT BE TRYING TO ACHIEVE.
	FOLLOWING THAT WE'VE TWO SESSIONS THAT WILL **DRAW ON YOUR READING**, AND ON WHAT WE'LL DO IN THE COURSE UP TO THAT POINT. WE'LL BE **THINKING** ABOUT AN '**IDEAL** SYSTEM'.
	THE **PRACTICE** SESSION WILL BE A VERY **BRIEF** '**VISIT**' to the **APPRAISAL INTERVIEW**. THERE REALLY WON'T BE MUCH TIME TO GO INTO THIS, BUT I THINK YOU'LL AGREE THAT INTERVIEWS CAN BE DIFFICULT, AND IT'S WORTH TAKING AN INITIAL LOOK TO FIND OUT MORE CERTAINLY 'WHY'.
	FINALLY THERE'LL BE THE OPPORTUNITY TO **PUT** ALL **THIS TOGETHER** AND **MAKE** SOME **DECISIONS** ABOUT WHAT HAS TO BE DONE – BY YOU, AND PERHAPS OTHERS. IT WILL GIVE YOU A 'ROLLING START' ON YOUR NEXT STAGE OF THE PROJECT.
	THAT'S A VERY QUICK 'TOUR' OF THE COURSE. **NOW** I'D LIKE TO **GET SOME REACTIONS** – SOME FEEDBACK **FROM YOU** ABOUT WHERE YOU ARE RIGHT NOW.

V3

COURSE OBJECTIVES

As a result of this course you will have:

- AGREED WITH YOUR SUBORDINATE MANAGERS AND YOUR COLLEAGUES HERE, THE PROBLEMS OF THE CURRENT PERFORMANCE APPRAISAL SYSTEM;

- AGREED WHAT NEEDS TO BE INCLUDED IN A NEW SYSTEM;

- DEVELOPED AN ACTION PLAN FOR 'HOW TO DO IT';

- AN ACTION PLAN TO IDENTIFY SUBORDINATES' TRAINING NEEDS.

Appendix C: Performance appraisal example

3

EXPECTATIONS AND OBJECTIVES

text	OK – WE'VE LOOKED THROUGH THE COURSE SCHEDULE AND THAT FLOW DIAGRAM OF HOW THINGS FIT TOGETHER. I'D LIKE YOU TO THINK ABOUT THAT FOR A SHORT WHILE. YOU HAVE SOME NOTEPAPER IN YOUR FOLDERS. I'D LIKE YOU TO **WRITE DOWN WHAT YOU EXPECT** FROM THIS **COURSE**. WHAT ARE THE **TWO OR THREE 'IMPORTANT OUTCOMES'** FOR YOU PERSONALLY THAT YOU HOPE TO ACHIEVE IN THE NEXT TWO DAYS? DON'T WORRY YOURSELF WITH A LOT OF DEPTH OR DETAIL. JUST TAKE A **COUPLE** OF **MINUTES** TO NOTE WHAT'S IN YOUR MIND RIGHT NOW.
note	Allow participants to complete their work. Ask each person for their 'wants'. Make a note of them, to be referred to during the course, and in the end-of-course review. Consider balance with objectives.
text	I KNOW YOU ALL HAD A COPY OF THE COURSE OBJECTIVES IN YOUR PRE-WORK. I'D LIKE YOU TO TAKE ANOTHER LOOK, AND WE CAN CHECK THESE AGAINST YOUR EXPECTATIONS.
V3	**Objectives**
note	Talk through the objectives, explaining how each element contributes, e.g. . . .
text	YOU'VE ALREADY DISCUSSED THE SYSTEM WITH YOUR OWN MANAGER AND TEAM. YOU'VE ALREADY COME TO SOME VIEW ABOUT PROBLEMS. **WE'LL 'FINISH OFF' THE FIRST OBJECTIVE** BY THE **END OF THE MORNING**. WE MIGHT 'POLISH' OR MODIFY OUR VIEWS AS WE MOVE A LITTLE DEEPER INTO THE COURSE. THIS **AFTERNOON'S SESSIONS** ON 'FACTORS' AND 'NEEDS' WILL SEE US ACHIEVE THE **SECOND OBJECTIVE**. FINALLY, AT THE **END OF THE SECOND DAY** YOU'LL BE DEALING WITH THE 'SO WHAT' OF THE PROCESS. YOU'LL BE DECIDING WHAT NEEDS TO BE DONE TO TAKE YOUR PROJECT TO THE NEXT STEPS. YOU'LL HAVE YOUR **ACTION PLANS**. OK – HOW DOES THAT BALANCE WITH YOUR EXPECTATIONS?
note	**Check again for balance between** participants' expectations of outcomes and those in the objectives. Where these are clearly at odds, discuss with relevant participants. **Attempt to bring** these **into balance**, if possible. Where the 'imbalance' appears to be widespread among the group, attempts should be made to modify elements of the programme. If this cannot be done, say so.

fp 4

PEOPLE HAVE A RIGHT TO THREE THINGS AT WORK

- TELL ME WHAT TO DO;
- GIVE ME THE TOOLS TO DO IT;
- TELL ME HOW I'M DOING.

WHY WE DO

- CAN BE TIED UP TO **PROMOTION**
- CAN HELP WITH PAY (RISES)
- TO **'MEASURE'** HOW WELL SOMEONE IS WORKING
- TO GIVE **'DISCIPLINED' FEEDBACK** TO PEOPLE ABOUT PERFORMANCE
- TO HELP **IDENTIFY** WHERE PEOPLE ARE HAVING **DIFFICULTY AT WORK**
- TO **MAKE SURE** MANAGERS AND SUBORDINATES *TALK* ABOUT 'PERFORMANCE'
- TO GIVE **CONSISTENCY IN** *MANAGING* **PERFORMANCE**
- CAN BE USED IN **CAREER PLANNING**
- CAN BE USED/TIED TO **TRAINING NEEDS ANALYSIS**
- CAN IDENTIFY AND **ISOLATE AREAS** OF **GOOD AND BAD PERFORMANCE**.

WHEN WE DON'T

- MORE **ARGUMENTS** ABOUT 'WHO IS BETTER' FOR PROMOTION
- **CONFRONTING** POOR PERFORMANCE IS **EASIER TO AVOID**
- APPRAISING PERFORMANCE CAN BECOME A SECRET PROCESS
- DISCUSSING PERFORMANCE CAN BECOME **TABOO**
- **PERFORMANCE CAN GO UNMANAGED**
- **PEOPLE** ARE LEFT **IN DOUBT** ABOUT HOW WELL THEY'RE WORKING
- PEOPLE ARE IN **MORE DOUBT** ABOUT HOW THEY CAN DEVELOP THEIR **CAREERS**
- MANAGERS AND SUBORDINATES **DON'T TALK ABOUT IMPORTANT THINGS** LIKE TRAINING NEEDS, CAREER ASPIRATIONS
- WHETHER PEOPLE 'GET ON' IN AN ORGANIZATION CAN BE MORE A MATTER OF **PERSONALITY RATHER THAN PERFORMANCE**
- PEOPLE BECOME **CONFUSED ABOUT CRITERIA** FOR PROMOTION, TRAINING, ETC.

Appendix C: Performance appraisal example

4

WHY USE AN APPRAISAL SYSTEM?

text

OK. LET'S GET STARTED ON THE MATERIAL. WHAT I'D LIKE US TO DO **FIRST** IS TO WORK OUT **WHY** AN ORGANIZATION ACTUALLY **WANTS AN APPRAISAL SYSTEM.** LET'S FACE IT, THEY ARE **ALWAYS** A **HASSLE** IN SOME WAY OR ANOTHER.

FOR MANY PEOPLE THEY SEEM TO BE ABOUT AS POPULAR AS A BAD SMELL IN AN ELEVATOR!

FORGET ABOUT OUR OWN PARTICULAR SYSTEM FOR NOW. FORGET ABOUT ANY PROBLEMS OR DIFFICULTIES YOU THINK THERE ARE.

JUST FOR **NOW** WE'RE GOING TO **'BRAINSTORM'** SOME IDEAS ABOUT **WHY** AN ORGANIZATION WOULD WANT OR NEED A PERFORMANCE APPRAISAL SYSTEM.

IF WE HAD A PERFECT SYSTEM, WHAT WOULD IT BE DOING FOR US?

LET'S GET AS MANY IDEAS UP ON THE BOARD AS WE CAN. DON'T BOTHER ABOUT WHETHER EVERYBODY AGREES WITH THEM YET.

DON'T MAKE ANY JUDGEMENTS ABOUT WHETHER THE IDEAS ARE ANY GOOD OR NOT. WE'LL DEAL WITH THAT LATER.

FOR NOW – WHY DO WE DO IT?

note

Use two flipcharts to record the group's ideas. One should be labelled **'Why we use one'**, the other **'What happens when we don't?'**

If participants are slow in starting up, offer **an example** or two **from the facing page**. Ensure that all of these examples are included in the group's final brainstorm list.

Make sure that any **'one word answers'** are **clearly understood** by expanding them where necessary. Seek agreement on meaning, not on whether it's 'right' or 'valuable'.

Appendix C: Performance appraisal example

5

REASONS – RELATIVE IMPORTANCE

text	OK – WE'VE GOT OUR LIST, AND WE HAVE SOME AGREEMENT ABOUT WHAT IT MEANS. WE HAVEN'T SAID ANYTHING ABOUT WHETHER WE **AGREE** WITH **WHAT'S ON THE LIST**.
	WHAT WE'LL DO **NOW** IS JUST THAT BUT IN A SLIGHTLY DIFFERENT WAY.
	WHENEVER YOU HAVE A JOB TO DO – A PROJECT SUCH AS THIS – YOU CAN BET YOUR BOOTS THAT THE **PROJECT** WILL BE **MORE COMPLEX** THAN YOU WOULD WISH, OR THAT YOU DON'T REALLY HAVE ENOUGH TIME TO GET IT DONE AS WELL AS YOU'D LIKE.
	THIS PROJECT ISN'T LIKELY TO BE MUCH DIFFERENT. SO WE **NEED** SOME **WAYS OF KEEPING IN MIND** THE **REALLY IMPORTANT** THINGS SO THAT YOU CAN MAKE SURE AT LEAST THESE GET ATTENTION.
	SO IT IS WITH THESE 'REASONS' WE'VE JUST LISTED. SOME ARE REALLY POWERFUL REASONS, SOME YOU MAY THINK ARE LESS IMPORTANT. WE'LL TALK ABOUT THAT NOW.
	WHICH SHOULD WE CONCENTRATE ON ACHIEVING FIRST WHEN DESIGNING A SYSTEM?
	WHAT WE'LL DO IS **NUMBER** THESE **1, 2, OR 3**.
	1 IS MOST IMPORTANT, 3 – LEAST. WHAT DO YOU THINK?
note	**Gather responses from the group**. Write in appropriate numbers as participants discuss and agree. Work to achieve as much agreement as time allows.
	As participants discuss their opinions, **ask 'why?'**
	When this is concluded, **attach the flipcharts/lists to** the **training room wall**.
text	**NOW** – BEFORE WE DISCUSS HOW OUR OWN SYSTEM MEASURES UP, I'D LIKE US TO DO A LITTLE MORE WORK. THIS TIME IN **SMALLER GROUPS**.

fp 6

SYNDICATE WORK – FEELINGS

(25 – 30 mins + 40)

Brief   Appraisal is an emotional event. The results can significantly affect your relationships with your boss, your progress, your motivation, your work.

How you *feel* just before, during and after your appraisal is conducted is clearly important to the way you approach your work, and of course, your ultimate performance.

Synd. 1 – How did **you feel** when . . .
Synd. 2 – How do you think **your subordinates feel** . . .

Examples

In pre-task brief – in synd. rooms with only one syndicate.

1   I was . . . before, because . . . while it was going on I felt . . . because . . .

She claimed . . . but didn't really know . . .. This made me feel . . . I actually . . .. Afterwards it was weeks before I . . ..

I don't feel good because I know that . . .. My boss . . .

2   I think they feel . . . when . . . because . . .

The result of . . . is . . ..

I get the impression that . . . because . . . this leads to . . ..

6

HOW DO PEOPLE FEEL ABOUT APPRAISAL?

text	WHAT WE'LL DO NOW IS BREAK INTO **TWO GROUPS** TO ANSWER A QUESTION. ACTUALLY THE QUESTION EACH GROUP IS ASKED IS MORE OR LESS THE SAME – BUT NOT QUITE. THE DIFFERENCE IS IMPORTANT, SO I'D LIKE YOU TO **MAKE SURE** THAT YOUR **'OPPOSING GROUP' DOESN'T SEE YOUR QUESTION**.
note	Break the group into two syndicates. Inform them where they will be working. Issue the syndicate briefs. Make sure syndicates see only one of the briefs.
HO	Syndicate task – '**How do they *feel* about *their* performance being appraised?**'
text	BY THE WAY, JUST BEFORE YOU GO OFF TO YOUR SYNDICATE AREAS IN ALL SYNDICATE TASKS I'D LIKE YOU **FIRST** TO SELECT SOMEONE TO **'CHAIR'** YOUR WORK – TO KEEP YOU ON TRACK AND ON TIME. AND YOU ALSO NEED TO GET SOMEONE ELSE TO ACT AS YOUR **'SCRIBE'**, TO WRITE ON YOUR FLIPCHARTS WHAT YOU HAVE AGREED. YOUR **CHAIRPERSON** WILL BE THE ONE WHO **REPORTS BACK** ON BEHALF OF YOUR SYNDICATE. I'D LIKE YOU TO **'ROTATE' THE ROLES** WITH EACH SYNDICATE EXERCISE. OK – CAN YOU GO TO YOUR SYNDICATE AREAS, AND ANSWER THE QUESTION? I'LL BE AROUND IN A LITTLE WHILE TO HELP YOU, IF YOU NEED IT. WE'LL GET BACK TOGETHER AGAIN IN **ABOUT TWENTY MINUTES**.
note	**Check** with syndicates to ensure **they understand** what they need to do. Try to help them use appropriate language (**emotion words**) to explain 'feelings'. If time is tight, help keep discussions brisk and to the point. Make sure that discussions are balanced by covering both **positive and negative feelings**. Have syndicates **avoid** any **judgement** as to whether feelings are reasonable or unreasonable, warranted or not. Just concentrate on feelings that are perceived to exist.

'FEELINGS OF APPRAISAL' – SYNDICATE DEBRIEFS

note	**Reconvene** syndicates after **twenty minutes**. Have them, display their flipcharts where the 'opposing group' can see them.
text	WHAT I'D LIKE TO DO **NOW** IS TO **COMPARE AND DISCUSS** YOUR RESPONSES. I'D LIKE US TO TALK ABOUT THE SITUATIONS YOU'VE EXPERIENCED THAT'S GIVEN RISE TO THE FEELINGS YOU'VE DESCRIBED.
	LET'S FACE IT – IN ANY **NEW SYSTEM** WE HAVE TO **AVOID** THINGS WHICH LEAVE US **FEELING NEGATIVE** ABOUT BEING APPRAISED, AND **INCORPORATE** EVERYTHING THAT IS LIKELY TO **MAKE US FEEL GOOD**.
	I'D LIKE US TO **EXPLORE** THE **DIFFERENCES** (OR OTHERWISE) BETWEEN THE TWO SYNDICATES' ANSWERS. THEY ARE LIKELY TO BE A BIT DIFFERENT SINCE ONE GROUP WAS ASKED ABOUT HOW THEY ACTUALLY FELT, AND THE OTHER GROUP – ABOUT HOW THEY THOUGHT YOUR SUBORDINATE MANAGERS FELT.
	IN **YOUR FEEDBACK** I'D LIKE YOU TO **TELL** US OF ANY **MAJOR DIFFERENCES** WITHIN **YOUR GROUP**.
	NOW REMEMBER, IT WILL BE VITALLY IMPORTANT TO THE SUCCESS OF YOUR OVERALL PROJECT THAT YOU CAN ELIMINATE AS MUCH OF THE NEGATIVES AS POSSIBLE. YOU WON'T BE ABLE TO DO THAT UNLESS YOU IDENTIFY THEM – SO **BE OPEN** WITH OUR DISCUSSIONS.
	WE WON'T BE TALKING 'SOLUTIONS' YET – WHAT COULD BE DONE BETTER, MORE OFTEN AND SO ON. WE'LL BE DISCUSSING THOSE THINGS LATER. FOR NOW, CONCENTRATE ONLY ON 'FEELINGS'.
note	Have syndicate chairpersons **quickly run through** their agreements. Intervene as needed to clarify or further explore the information.
	Check – are senior managers and their subordinates perceived to feel different/the same? Are perceptions and assumptions made realistic.
	Conclude by agreeing and **recording a 'consensus view'** of how people feel. Post flipcharts on wall.

fp 8

SYNDICATE EXERCISE

- Discuss outcomes of discussions with subordinate managers. Views similar among them re strengths and weaknesses? Their views similar to senior managers?
- Agree and list **strengths and weaknesses of current system**.
- Be prepared to explain why. **Cite actual events** to support your views.

Note:

CHECK ALL PREVIOUS FLIPCHARTS.

DOES FEEDBACK ON STRENGTHS AND WEAKNESSES REFLECT WHAT HAS BEEN AGREED ABOUT WHY WE USE A SYSTEM?

ARE THE STRENGTHS REFLECTING POSITIVES AND VICE VERSA?

IF NOT – WHY NOT?

Appendix C: Performance appraisal example

8

THE CURRENT SYSTEM

text	LET' **NOW** GET DOWN TO DEALING WITH THE **DISCUSSIONS YOU HAD WITH YOUR MANAGERS BEFORE** THE COURSE – THOSE RELATING SPECIFICALLY TO THE CURRENT PERFORMANCE APPRAISAL SYSTEM.
	THE WAY WE'RE GOING TO DO THIS IS ONCE AGAIN TO BREAK INTO **SYNDICATES** – THIS TIME **THREE**.
	IN THESE SMALLER SYNDICATES WE'RE GOING TO **DISCUSS** THE **STRENGTHS AND WEAKNESSES** OF THE **CURRENT SYSTEM**, IN TERMS OF THE OPINIONS YOU'VE FORMED AS A RESULT OF YOUR DISCUSSIONS.
HO	**Syndicate task** – Strengths and weaknesses of the current system
note	Issue the syndicate brief, and talk through, ensuring understanding. Inform groups of their syndicate arrangements.
text	IN YOUR SYNDICATES I'D LIKE YOU TO **TALK ABOUT WHAT HAPPENED** WHEN YOU **DISCUSSED** THE PRESENT **SYSTEM WITH** YOUR **SUBORDINATE MANAGERS**.
	WHAT DID **THEY SAY?** WHAT DID **YOU THINK?**
	WERE VIEWS DIFFERENT BETWEEN YOU, OR BETWEEN DIFFERENT MANAGERS YOU SPOKE TO? WERE THERE ANY SURPRISES?
	WHEN YOU'VE DONE THIS I'D LIKE YOU TO **AGREE A LIST** OF THE **STRENGTHS AND WEAKNESSES** OF THE SYSTEM AS YOU NOW SEE IT.
	WE'LL GET TOGETHER IN ANOTHER **30 MINUTES** OR SO TO CHECK ON THE RESULTS.
note	Keep in touch with syndicate discussions. Get **them** to **note specific reasons** for their initial view of strengths and weaknesses. Try to determine whether or not senior managers are genuinely taking into account their subordinate managers' views, or whether they are tending to hold or form still different views, for whatever reason.
	Be prepared to discuss this.
	Reconvene in 30 minutes.
	When reconvened, explore the syndicates' discussions and outputs. Identify where individuals and syndicates differed. Discuss the ramifications of any differences. **Agree a final list of strengths and weaknesses**.

Appendix C: Performance appraisal example

9

REVIEW SO FAR

text

OK. WE'VE TALKED ABOUT WHY ORGANIZATIONS, INCLUDING US, USE PERFORMANCE APPRAISAL SYSTEMS. AND WE'VE TALKED ABOUT HOW PEOPLE – YOU AND YOUR MANAGERS – SEEM TO FEEL ABOUT IT. HOW IT SEEMS TO IMPACT ON YOU RIGHT NOW.

WE'VE NOW JUST LOOKED AT WHAT WE THINK ARE THE GOOD POINTS AND THE BAD POINTS ABOUT THE SYSTEM WE'RE USING.

THIS AFTERNOON WE'RE GOING TO WORK WITH THE **INFORMATION** YOU HAVE, AND THE **OPINIONS** YOU WOULD HAVE FORMED FROM YOUR **READINGS** ABOUT PERFORMANCE APPRAISAL **BEFORE THE COURSE**.

WE'LL THEN MOVE ON TO IDENTIFYING WHAT WE MIGHT LIKE TO SEE IN ANY FUTURE APPRAISAL SYSTEM.

BEFORE WE DO THOUGH – LET'S MAKE SURE WE KNOW WHAT WE'VE ALREADY GONE THROUGH, AND FORM SOME SORT OF IDEA ABOUT HOW THAT WILL MATCH IN WITH THE WORK WE'RE GOING TO DO A LITTLE LATER.

TAKE A **LOOK AT** THE **FLIPCHARTS** WE'VE PRODUCED. WHAT DO THEY TELL US ABOUT THE PROBLEMS WE SEEM TO NEED TO RESOLVE?

note

Work with participants to **identify and briefly discuss** the **problems as perceived** by addressing the outputs of the first three exercises:

- **Reasons for appraisal**
- **Feelings**
- **Strengths and weaknesses.**

Clearly attending to the negatives or downsides of the three exercises should indicate problem areas.

Record agreements about **problems to be solved on flipcharts**. Attach finished flips to walls alongside all previous flipcharts.

Well – there it is. I feel better about it. After investing some more time and thought I have a product that now gives me a surer feel of pace and drama. The squint tests work out better. (Not on every page, it is true, but by and large . . .)

I have nine pages of text to take me through a morning. I am much more comfortable with that now. Any more and I would be well into the waffle stage. As it is, it is easy to recognize this is not 'input intensive'.

Most of the reading that participants would have done before the course eliminates the need for a conventional 'lecture'. When it comes to the afternoon there will be a greater need for input, but not now.

I still have plenty of natural breaks. (My page titles tell me that.) My timetable, which I will show after these comments, also gives me plenty of information about pace.

I was right in assuming I would need more time for the introduction and administration material. I think my rewrite allows my participants to settle down more. I have slowed down a lot. They will have time to breath, and feel more positive about being away from their normal place of work. Text page 1 leaves participants with a clearer indication that there will be a practical output from their two-day investment.

Text page 2 is the 'tell 'em what you're going to tell 'em' page. That is always a good idea, isn't it? The logic of events is being shown here.

I know we are not bothered with actual content in these pages, but as a small aside, I think it is always worthwhile to pin people down on what they expect. It helps to focus them early on. It also gives the trainer a chance to modify the material if needed, or at least to reshape expectations about what is actually going to happen.

In text 3 it is a matter of negotiating 'the realities'. If expectations are well out of line with objectives I will have to decide on either a 'hard line approach', or determine whether their expectations can be met with some modifications. What I do will depend on many factors, including how idiosyncratic differences in expectations are. My format will tell me much about the impact of potential modifications.

All in all I have not really made many changes. I have managed to find more space and spaces to help me pick up information quickly. I have plenty of facing page space on which to write the notes I will need as I go through the course.

The questions I asked myself after the first draft have forced me into better visualization of the process. I now feel confident that I can control the direction, time and the quality of outputs.

Does it work better for you?

The timetable follows. Take a look to see how it all comes together.

Appendix C: Performance appraisal example

T	V/HO		min	end time	notes
		Start		9.00	
1		Administration and introduction	5		
2	**V2**	Course structure		9.05	
3	V3	Expectations and objectives	10	9.15	
4		Why use an appraisal system?	15	9.30	
5		Reasons – relative importance	10	9.40	
6	**HO**	How do people feel – **synd.** ex.	20	10.00	
7		Syndidate debrief	30	10.30	
		Break	15	**10.45**	

8	**HO**	The current system
		    Synd. Ex
		    Brief 5
		    Task 30
		    Debrief 30
			65	11.50	

9		Review so far	10	12.00	
		Lunch	60	1.00	
10		xxxxxxxxxxxxxxxxxx			
11		vvvvvvvvvvvvvvvvv			

Index

appraisal interviews, 40, 44–5

course presentation,
   on performance appraisal, 111–31
   on quality customer service, 105–10

documentation, value, 2

improvisation, drawbacks, 2–3

Mager, R, 14, 24, 69
mind maps,
   performance appraisal, 35
   time management, 49

performance appraisal, 73–7
   action planning, 41–2, 45
   appraisal interviews, 40, 44–5
   course content summary, 35–7, 42–5
   course objectives, 25–6
   course orientation, 37–8
   course presentation, 111–31
   course rationale, 23, 24, 28
   mind map, 35
   and performance management, 39, 44
   pre-course tasks, 36
   sample text, 73, 78–9, 80–8
performance management, 39, 44
Preparing Instructional Objectives, 14, 24, 69
presentation techniques, sample text, 68–72, 95–103, 112–31

quality customer service,
   course content summary, 47–8
   course presentation, 105–10
   course rationale, 30–2
   objections to, 47
   sample text, 72–3, 74–7, 105–10

role playing, 40

syndicate exercises, 37, 38–9, 40, 41, 43, 51, 52

time management,
   course content summary, 50–2
   course objectives, 26, 50
   course rationale, 23–4, 29
   mind map, 48–9
   pre-course tasks, 50–1
timetables,
   examples, 53, 54, 56, 131
   as publicity, 53
   value of, 53, 55, 57
training,
   correct approach, 14–15
   effectiveness, 3
   process, 34
training courses,
   action planning, 41–2
   administration, 37
   approach, 27
   consistency, 9
   course orientation, 37–8
   customer definition, 22
   design, 34
   duration, 21–2
   effectiveness, 3–4
   and entertainment, 13
   equipment, 57–8
   goals, 25
   introductory text, 22–4
   objectives, 11, 14–15, 24–7
   outline, 7
   planning, 34
   pre-course tasks, 27, 36
   preparation, 3–4, 91–2
   presentation, 96–103
   promotion, 15

psychology, 14
purpose, 24
rationale, 19–28, 46
   examples, 28–32
review, 93
syndicate exercises, 38–9
title, 19, 21
wider needs, 40
training manual,
   approaches to writing, 1–3
   common format, 12–13
   content summary, 33–4, 42–5, 47–8, 50–2
   guidelines, 9–14
   language, 11–12
   lists, 57–8
   miscellaneous material, 90
   problems of writing, 11
   structure, 15–18
   style, 11–12
   summary, 8
   support documentation, 89
   text,
      examples, 64–7
      guidelines, 60–3
      value of, 59–60
   timetable, 53–7
   use, 91–3
   value, ix–x
   writing,
      guidelines, 9–14
      sequence, 11
      stages, 7–8
training objectives,
   defining, 14–15
   examples, 2